THE COMPLETE BOOK OF
MAKING MINIATURES

OTHER BOOKS BY THELMA R. NEWMAN

Wax as Art Form
Plastics as an Art Form
Plastics as Design Form
Creative Candlemaking
Contemporary Decoupage
Leather as Art and Craft
Plastics as Sculpture
Paper as Art and Craft
The Frame Book
Contemporary African Arts and Crafts
Quilting, Patchwork, Applique, and Trapunto

All photographs by the authors
unless otherwise noted.

THE COMPLETE BOOK OF MAKING MINIATURES

FOR ROOM SETTINGS AND DOLLHOUSES

by THELMA R. NEWMAN
and VIRGINIA MERRILL

Crown Publishers, Inc., New York

To: *Jay and Lee*
Susan and Peter

Inquiries should be addressed to Crown Publishers, Inc., One Park Avenue, New York, N.Y. 10016.

Printed in the United States of America Published simultaneously in Canada by General Publishing Company Limited

Library of Congress Cataloging in Publication Data

Newman, Thelma R
    The complete book of making miniatures.

    Bibliography: p.
    Includes index.
    1. Doll-houses. 2. Miniature rooms.
I. Merrill, Virginia, joint author. II. Title.
TT175.3.N48 1975   646.4'3'04   75–16456
ISBN 0–517–52318–3
ISBN 0-517-524600 pbk

Fourth Printing, August, 1976

ACKNOWLEDGMENTS

A complete book such as this owes its existence to countless people who have contributed to the miniature arts in the past and present. Many Individuals, museums, collectors, and companies helped us. The information and work gathered here could never have been compiled without their generous cooperation.

Very special thanks goes to Ed Leonard, Paul A. Runyon, Eugene Kupjack, Donald C. Buttfield, Elizabeth Scull, Frederick Hicks, Deborah McKnight, Jean Jessop, David Dorsi, Carol Dinkel, Jeanne Knoop, William Weder, Eleanor McCown, Mary C. Brady, Mary Jane Graham, Harry Smith, Robert Bernhard, and Jan Burton for sharing their expertise with us.

We also are most appreciative of June C. Stocks of the Suffolk Museum and Carriage House, as well as the curators of museum collections throughout the world. Catherine MacLaren, editor of the *Nutshell News* was also a veritable gold mine of information.

Our thanks as well to Gloria Hurme and Susan Richardson for sharing their hands in our step-by-step photographs, to Norm Smith for his first-rate film processing, and to Patricia Weidner for her gal Friday activities.

Lastly, our very special gratitude goes to our husbands for their cooperation and patience.

T.R.N.
V.M.

CONTENTS

In small proportions we just beauties see;
And in short measures, life may perfect be.

—Ben Jonson

PREFACE

There is no doubt that building, assembling, and collecting miniatures expresses a love of precision and a passion for detail. The range of expertise required to create miniature environments is vast because it traverses almost every craft known to humans from blowing glass to throwing a pot, weaving, all the way to building furniture and houses. All of this is converted to scale with mathematical exactness.

It is toward these ends that this book was written. The authors hope that the introductions to a broad range of craftsmanship with many different kinds of materials will involve the miniature environment-maker in creating and in understanding the skills implicit in these various areas.

When translations from materials bog down, improvisation fills in as a necessity. It is this exercise of imagination that challenges and stimulates. There are no final solutions for every possibility in *The Complete Book of Making Miniatures,* just ways to get going, presented conceptually and kept open-ended, inasmuch as the artist-craftsman must put something personal into his or her expression.

If *The Complete Book of Making Miniatures* provides concrete information that is genuinely helpful, that is gratifying because we told all we could in the allotted space; but if the range of possibility presented here inspires, then we feel that we have reached our ultimate goal.

In the advent that certain craft areas excite you to go on, we have provided further references in books, supply sources, people, organizations, and periodicals where one can find additional information and help.

Certainly the miniature world encompasses a maximum of skill and knowledge.

T.R.N.
V.M.

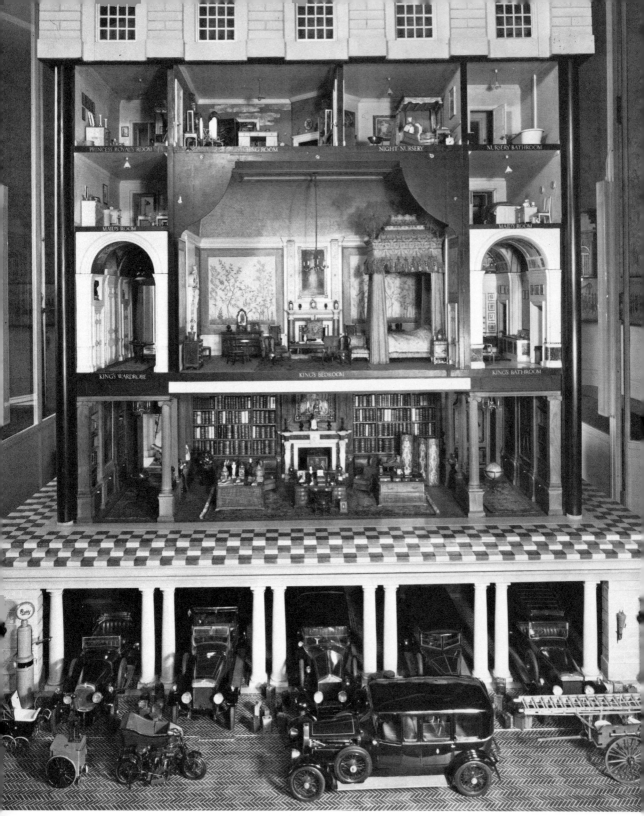

Queen Mary's Dolls' House is an early 20th-century monument to miniaturization. This is but one cut-away view of a precise and gigantic effort. *Courtesy: Lord Chamberlain, St. James's Palace, London*

1 | SOMETHING ABOUT MINIATURES

Smallness has charm. There is something precious and appealing about the precise detail of a minute thing. Although small things rarely have risen high in the eyes of art critics, the smallness of objects has enchanted mankind throughout the ages. Perhaps it is people's love for precision. Or it may be that smallness awakens a nostalgia harkening a person back to childhood, reviving one's instincts for play, for visiting the mysterious and imaginative world of pretend.

But the miniature world is more than that—it depicts in microcosm man's values and life-styles. These are records, little historical monuments. The Egyptians created small dolls illustrating all occupations and pastimes of their civilization. The Greeks also made objects of glass and other materials which were classified as toys. But often as not, they were playthings of adults, not children. The Chinese, Indians, and Japanese also mirrored in miniature aspects of their societies, as did Westerners. Glassblowers of Murano in Venice produced little things in the Middle Ages. One fantastic monument to miniaturization that detailed every aspect of gracious early twentieth-century living was Queen Mary's dollhouse. Earlier the seventeenth- and eighteenth-century Dutch and Germans left behind remarkable records of their envi-

1

ronments in miniature. Scores of artists and craftsmen from all over the world, working in every medium, have created as *tours de force,* tiny replicas of their full-sized creations.

In many societies today, as well as in the past, people have replicated themselves in miniature by dressing their children in small duplication of their own clothing. Indeed, children became living "dolls." We see this recorded in paintings of the past. And today, people of many Amerindian societies dress their children in child-sized versions of their own clothes.

Children's clothes, in turn, are duplicated in even smaller form for dolls. Some are very sophisticated indeed and so precious that they are not created for children but for adults who collect them. Craftsmen in almost every country in the world make dolls, depicting in miniature their costumes and occupations.

Dolls, too, need houses, furnishings, and pretend food. So houses were built for the child's make-believe world, except that these houses also

Many societies mirrored miniature aspects of their life-styles. This is a 19th-century Chinese lacquer on tortoise cabinet with Paktong hardware. It is a second-size piece which is an inbetween size that varies from piece to piece. *Collection of Jeanne Knoop*

Ribbon glass bowl, Roman Empire circa
1st century B.C. to 1st century A.D. Depth 8.7
cm (.01 cm is .39 inch) or 3.43 inches. *Courtesy: The Corning Museum of Glass*

Dark blue glass flask with yellow and
white thread decoration in form of a lotus
column made by the core technique. Egyptian, 18th Dynasty. Height 8.5 cm, or 3.32
inches. *Courtesy: The Corning Museum of
Glass*

People all over the world replicated themselves in miniature. These figures are wax carved with cloth impregnated
with wax from Oaxaca, Mexico. Height, approximately 2
1/2 to 3 inches.

4

Miniatures from Surinam, South America, made of natural latex.

A hand-carved and painted wooden figure from Thailand. Height, approximately 3 inches.

5

The popular dolls' houses of the 17th and 18th centuries Netherlands were not playthings for children. This is a "best" kitchen, as opposed to a "cooking" kitchen (where cooking is done). The dome in the ceiling is designed in an octagonal pattern and painted in *trompe l'œil* style. The contents of the hand-painted cabinets contain all costly things. This remarkable house was made for Petronella Dortman who married Johannes Brandt in 1686. Height, 52 cm or 30.68 inches. *Courtesy: The Rijksmuseum, Amsterdam*

Some glass from the best kitchen. Height: 5.2–6.5 cm, or 2 to 2 1/2 inches. *Courtesy: The Rijksmuseum, Amsterdam*

Porcelain china from the best kitchen. Height: 5 cm or about 2 inches. *Courtesy: The Rijksmuseum*

became so precise and precious that they were deeded to adults for their own amusement. Indeed, the dollhouses of seventeenth- and eighteenth-century Netherlands and Germany were never intended as playthings for children. Their contents were too costly. Besides, seeking out and gathering small things did not take up too much space and did satisfy people's passion for collecting. How many of us know of today's fathers who bought complicated miniature trains as presents for their children, set them up in elaborate topologically correct environments, and then proceeded to play with the trains themselves?

Play notwithstanding, people have always been curious about distant worlds. Distance miniaturizes (but makes for blurr, loss of detail and color). Distance can also be very close, in the invisible world of the microscopic. In order to see more and more, ever more precisely, man developed lenses that could peer into the unknown, into the distant worlds of the macrocosmic as well as the microcosmic. This quest for seeing the smallest of particles has progressed through a multitude of inventions and discoveries to the electronic age. Miniaturization today is raised to remarkable heights in the computers and calculators we are using, coming a long way from the writing of the Lord's Prayer on the head of a pin. The electronic age has dwarfed the achievements of a London banker, Mr. Peters, who in a paper read before the Microscopi-

Peoples' passion for collecting miniature things seems to have intensified over the years. Here is a contemporary carousel by Brilar that is a precise and expensive adult "toy." *Collection of Elizabeth Ellis*

cal Society of London in 1855, described a machine he had invented that made it possible for him to write the Lord's Prayer, without any abbreviations, in a space under 1/150,000th of a square inch. Seven years later, he improved his machine so that the same text could be written in a space of 1/356,000th of a square inch—very small indeed!

Microphotography today can significantly reduce the printed work to readable size, with use of magnifying glasses, of course. The twelve volumes of the *Oxford English Dictionary* are reproduced micrographically in two volumes. Magnitudes of writing are encapsulated on plastic film in microfilm storage and retrieval systems.

Synthetic materials also introduce new dimensions. Molds can be made of RTV silicone for casting tiny forms in glasslike and metal-like plastics. Weaving can be so miniaturized that blood vessels can be woven of Dacron so finely and closely that blood will not seep through. (These vessels also are heat formed into an accordion-pleated tube so they can expand and contract as the heart pumps blood through these synthetic arteries and veins.) This is modest, though, compared to the awesome fact that *miniaturization made it possible for man to visit the moon.*

Miniature can be small, very small, or microscopic, depending on one's reference point. The word itself comes from the Italian *miniare,* which meant to dye, paint, or color with lead. The word *minatura* then evolved to describe the very small, detailed paintings of illuminated

Size standards for miniatures have varied enormously. This is a hand-carved ivory cabinet from Mexico that is only two inches high.

And this Mexican kitchen cabinet of wood with ceramic, glass, straw, and cloth elements is 6 1/2 inches high.

You can judge this El Salvador plaster of Paris miniature (that is usually covered by the swan) by the size of a normal match-folder match in the right foreground.

A miniature folk art cabinet from Peru is a folk art tradition. The ceramic figures depict scenes from their life. The interior height of the cabinet measures 11 1/4 inches and the tallest figure is 3 inches.

This is called a "second-size" piece, dating from the 18th century. The corner chair, from Pennsylvania or New Jersey, is made of walnut and measures 7 3/4 inches high, 7 inches deep with a 4 3/4 inch square seat. *Courtesy: Philadelphia Museum of Art. Bequest of Henrietta Morris Bonsal*

An American 18th-century tilt-top table made of mahogany measuring 4 1/2 inches high (untilted) and 4 1/2 inches deep. *Courtesy: Philadelphia Museum of Art. Bequest of Henrietta Morris Bonsal*

manuscripts. Usually these medieval book illustrations were painted in vermillion or red lead and then overlayed with gold leaf. Miniature paintings escaped the book into their own "world," along with miniature sculptures, often modeled in beeswax.

Standards of size, called "miniature," vary enormously from child-sized objects to dollhouse objects for the doll's world, here too varying in dimension, to replicas in small size of craftsman's products that fitted into the traveling salesman's carrying cases. These cabinet-maker's samples ranged from 5 inches to 40 inches high and appeared in every style from Renaissance to late Victorian. But the standard today for miniature settings of one-twelfth of a foot (one inch to one foot) has appeared proportionally throughout the ages to be reaffirmed by collectors and miniature-makers today.

Curiously, Jonathan Swift in *Gulliver's Travels* has Lemuel Gulliver describe Lilliput in what can be translated as approximately one inch to one foot! Among other indicators, Gulliver says, after entering the courtyard of the Lilliputians' Royal Palace, "Lying on my side, I ap-

A second-size Empire period mahogany table with ivory trim made in 1840. The doll collection is in miniature as well. *Collection of Jeanne Knoop*

This English circa 1800 satinwood and mahogany demi-commode is a second-size piece. *Collection of Jeanne Knoop*

A primitive boxed miniature from Mexico. Note that the ceramic figures are out of proportion to the sizes of the table, chair, and plates.

plied my face to the windows of the middle storeys and discovered the most splendid apartments that can be imagined. ... Her Imperial Majesty was pleased to smile very graciously upon me, and give me out of the window her hand to kiss." We can project, if Gulliver's human mouth was over two inches long, and his eye, which was less than two inches wide, could just peer into a window, then the Empress's hand was, at the very most, one-quarter inch in length. Gulliver also found a "young girl threading an invisible needle with invisible silk." Queen Mary's Dolls' House, which was designed by Sir Edwin Lutyens, was also based on a 1/12th to an inch scale. So are Mrs. Thorne's 68 remarkable rooms that reside in the Art Institute of Chicago.

With these outstanding examples proportioned to a 1/12th to an inch scale, and many others following this precedent over the years, there developed a tacit movement to standardize miniatures based on common measurements. So many old examples of miniature rooms look ludicrous when objects of various scale sizes have been placed in the same space. The effect is almost primitive. A two inches to the foot cup may be resting on a table scaled one-half inch to the foot, and the texture of a rug sample, in actual size covering a floor, may clash with the one-inch to the foot scale of everything else in the room. The effect is crude and is okay for child's play but is not acceptable for the collector and craftsman.

Yet another standard for miniatures exists, this is in the area of miniature trains where standardization happened earlier because it was more critical. The "O" scale is 1/4-inch to the foot and the "HO" scale is 3 1/2mm to the foot or 1/87th of actual size. So a miniature

The comparative measure of this HO scale passenger car model by Robert K. Aaberg is 1/87th of the actual size or 1/8 inch to the foot. *Courtesy: Robert K. Aaberg and Railroad Model Craftsman Copyright 1974 Carstens Publications*

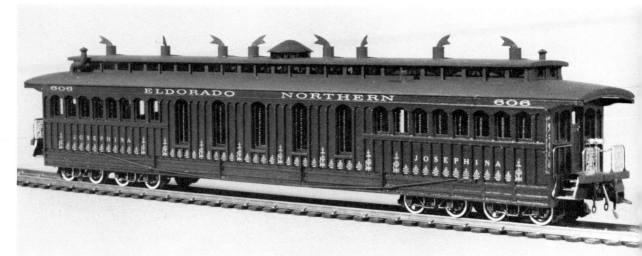

The "Josephina" was the director's car of the C&NW Railroad and originally was built in 1867 by Henry Hull. Only the names and filigree details have been changed on the exterior. *Courtesy: Robert K. Aaberg and Railroad Model Craftsman*

A bird's-eye view of the plush interior complete with carpeting, wall decorations, mirrors, and furniture. *Courtesy: Robert K. Aaberg and Railroad Model Craftsman*

This is a central view of the filigree detailed ceiling and dome of the car. Gold filigree ribbons were cut into fine strips to form the border around the ceiling. Costume jewelry items constitute the brass light fixtures. *Courtesy: Robert K. Aaberg and Railroad Model Craftsman*

house created on a one-inch to the foot scale cannot be successfully combined with miniature trains.

Fortunately, there are examples of miniature settings created with high standards and precise attention paid to the most obscure details. The Queen's Dolls' House is one. Even the thickness of paint was reduced in proportion. Scores of artists working together developed this masterpiece. The Queen's Dolls' House (now at Windsor Castle) is one of the most remarkable collections of authentic miniature rooms ever produced. The architecture pays tribute to the spirit of Sir Christopher Wren but the house itself, created for the queen's amusement, was more of a symbol of her domesticity. Queen Mary was always a home-body figure and paid extraordinary importance to the small details of life. Hence, this significative piece of art.

The house itself, started in the spring of 1921, is a balance between tradition and innovation. On the main it is 116 inches long, 72 inches wide, and 39 inches high, and consists of 208 interchangeable drawers, half on the north and half on the south side, covered by falling flap doors made of cedar and fitted with a drop ring handle of ivory.

In the base is a basement containing transformers to convert the normal electric circuit to four volts, as well as switches, and water arrangements to pump and receive water from bath, toilets, and sinks. In addition, the basement contains a wine cellar with honeycomb walls holding over 100 dozen bottles of wine. Nearby is a storage area for groceries and a garage containing six cars.

It is a symmetrical house containing a grand staircase hall and lobbies on the ground floor. In the kitchen, the wood block floor consists of 2,000 tiny sections of oak. There is also a strong room and safe to house the crown jewels. And elevators travel from basement to the top

This is the library of Queen Mary's Dolls' House. Every book, bound in leather and embossed with gold leaf decoration, is readable. Paintings and sculptures were created by well-known artists of the day. *Courtesy: Lord Chamberlain, St. James's Palace, London*

KING'S BEDROOM

Every piece of furniture in Queen Mary's Dolls' House is a 1/12th-inch to the foot working version of an authentic piece. Drawers open, door handles close, and clocks tick. This is the king's bedroom. *Courtesy: Lord Chamberlain, St. James's Palace, London*

floor. Even the carpets are made with as many warp and weft threads as would be required to carpet a full-size room.

It took three years to construct the Queen's Dolls' House. No wonder, for even the piano is equipped with a soundboard, a cast steel frame, strings, hammers, ivory and ebony keys, which would make music with tinkling small sounds if there were hands small enough to play the instrument.

Paintings and sculptures were made by well-known artists of the day. Even the library contains thousands of readable volumes of literature. All books are bound in leather and embossed with gold leaf decoration. Some are as small as 3/4 inch by 1/2 inch. (A book was written just to annotate the library's contents.)

There are no dolls in the Queen's Dolls' House except the king and queen. The guards and pipe major reside outside. All other inhabitants would cause a risk. They could fall and break things.

There have been other elegant dollhouses. The Nostell Priory dollhouse, built in 1735 by Robert Adam, was furnished by Chippendale (who was an apprentice at that time). Beside Chippendale, Sheraton and other famous furniture makers were involved in creating dollhouses and some of their furnishings. Architects then and now often design

The queen's bedroom is complete down to the cosmetics containers on the dressing table. Even the rug is woven to scale. *Courtesy: Lord Chamberlain, St. James's Palace, London*

Water runs into the marble tub and into the marble-topped sinks in the king's bathroom of Queen Mary's Dolls' House. It is almost impossible to discern, in a photograph, that everything is in 1/12-inch scale and not a full-scale example. *Courtesy: Lord Chamberlain, St. James's Palace, London*

A Chippendale display cabinet in walnut. Made in the 19th century. *Collection of Jeanne Knoop*

and sometimes construct models of houses. Queen Anne gave a costly dollhouse to her godchild Ann Sharp (circa 1700) and Cardinal Richelieu presented a miniature room to the Duc de Maine. Early English dollhouses were very crude until after the Restoration. Then Charles II returned with his court from exile in Holland and brought with him a taste for a higher quality of miniatures. After that there was a notable improvement in English miniatures.

The very elegant miniature houses that inspired Charles II's court can be seen in the Rijksmuseum, Amsterdam, dating back to 1676. One collection belonged to Margaretha de Ruyter. A great variety of treatments can be seen there. Houses are paneled in rosewood, contain precisely made furniture, silver, and porcelain. One Amsterdam silversmith, Christiaan Waarenberg, forged a miniature silver urn, a replica of a full-sized one. (Both can be viewed in the Rijksmuseum.) The Leenwarden Silversmiths of Friesland (Netherlands) made silver miniature objects as early as the fifteenth century, continuing their output through the seventeenth century. Tea sets, vases, trays, bowls,

French Battersea chairs, enamel and ormolu in 1/12-inch scale. *Collection of Susan Richardson*

candlesticks, even furniture, ships, sleighs, and coaches were miniaturized in silver. This tradition has spread to the making of workable, movable, miniature charms in gold and silver for women's charm bracelets.

A collection of antique miniatures in silver. *Collection of
Elizabeth Ellis*

Miniatures in brass. *Collection of Jeanne Knoop*

A group of lacy pressed-glass miniatures made in the
United States somewhere around 1835–1850. *Courtesy: The
Corning Museum of Glass*

"The Royal Wedding Breakfast" is in sterling except for rugs of gold and silver. *Produced in 1934 by Edward Biggs & Co., England*

Antique enameled bronze boy and cart. *Collection of Virginia Merrill*

Although by this time dolls' houses were de-dolled, Colleen Moore dramatizes the proportionate sizes in her Fairy Castle courtyard. *Courtesy: Chicago Museum of Science and Industry*

In America, two sisters were given a Christmas present (circa 1890), a gift of a dollhouse. After playing with it for many years, the then dilapidated dollhouse was stored away. Many years later, when those little girls were grandmothers, they decided to restore it and convert their toy into a fine Georgian Colonial home to be presented to the Western Reserve Historical Society. Everything was made by hand, to scale. Special tools were devised to construct furnishings. Many hours of research, planning, and designing resulted in the finely woven silk and lace curtains, rugs, and all the fine appointments. With this new elegance, the dolls were moved out.

Attempts to domicile dolls have existed, no doubt, over their 5,000-year history, but the de-dolling of dollhouses happened only when dolls became dangerous creatures, capable of crashing into and breaking precious art objects. Box and cabinet rooms emerged, doll-less, to display valuable miniatures. Fabergé created some miniatures with flowers that were boxed in settings. And it has been said that the Princess Augusta Dorothea of Schwarzburg-Arnstadt was the first collector of boxed rooms. A village house interior was attributed as the first boxed room that she collected.

But miniature crèche scenes of the Nativity were made in Naples, Italy, as early as the Middle Ages and have flourished ever since. These were box scenes.

Remarkable standards were established for the miniature setting in the early twenties when Mrs. James Ward Thorne saw the need and a

In the Bingham dollhouse, which is a Georgian Colonial home 3 feet 1 inch high, 3 feet 4 inches wide and 5 feet 8 inches deep, we find a downstairs drawing room, a long hallway leading to a dining room with bay windows, and a kitchen. Upstairs there is a master bedroom, nursery, hallway, and bath. The scale is 1 1/4 inch to the foot. Everything is precise, even to the readable books in the Sheraton cherry bookcases. The mahogany grand piano was made in Switzerland and plays Mozart's "Lullaby." Florence Osborne, an interior decorator, helped direct the reconstruction and the skilled craftsmen of the Jastromb Art Furniture Company of Cleveland, Ohio, made most of the furniture. *Courtesy: Western Reserve Historical Society*

way to record, install, and reconstruct period rooms. Two series of miniature rooms, one showing 37 American and another describing European interiors as well as one Chinese and one Japanese interior throughout five centuries (sixteenth to twentieth century) were created in 68 settings. Mrs. Thorne planned and supervised the making of these historically accurate records by a group of specially trained craftsmen. She also designed all the textile work, the curtains, some rugs, and upholstery. All rooms were built on a 1/12th" scale. Whereas for the European rooms, Mrs. Thorne collected most of the miniature objects over many years, in the American series, she had pieces custom made, to scale. In order to attain a consistency of size, special variations in processes were necessary. It took over a decade to work out problems

The Thorne rooms are other remarkable examples of the miniature arts. This is a ballroom in a Charleston, South Carolina house existing between 1775 and 1835. *Courtesy: Thorne American Rooms in Miniature, The Art Institute of Chicago*

This Thorne room is an entrance hall of a Carter's Grove house (James City County, Virginia), circa 1751. Every part is duplicated to perfection in 1/12 inch scale. *Courtesy: Thorne American Rooms in Miniature, The Art Institute of Chicago*

Another room designed by Mrs. James Ward Thorne; this one, a parlor in a "Middletown" house that may have existed between 1875 and 1900. *Courtesy: Thorne American Rooms in Miniature, The Art Institute of Chicago*

Mrs. Thorne paid meticulous attention to every detail and had the work carried out under her supervision, although she created some of the textiles, rugs, upholstery, and curtains. This is a Wilton, Henrico County, Virginia 1754 drawing room. *Courtesy: Thorne American Rooms in Miniature, The Art Institute of Chicago*

An English Cotswold Cottage interior by Eugene Kupjack complete with a "flickering" fireplace, half-hidden stairway, leather upholstered wing chair, gateleg table, and Windsor chair, among other authentic appointments including a bobbin lace-making stand.

Another Eugene Kupjack interior in 1/12-inch scale. This French Louis XV (1740–60) drawing room is typical of a room of that period. The floor is real parquet. The fabric covering the three chairs is from a piece of 1750 French dress fabric. The fireplace is made of Sienna marble; walls are painted in the hue of "French putty"; gold accents are all created with gold leaf. The portrait is a miniature copy of Reynolds's "Lady Hamilton."

and complete the job. So accurate are these settings that they appear to be theatre scenes where Lilliputian players are participating. All one needs is a bit of imagination. It is worth a visit to the Art Institute of Chicago to see these.

One artist who worked on some of Mrs. James Ward Thorne's rooms was Eugene Kupjack. He has continued this work and still creates most elegant traditional settings. A notable series by Mr. Kupjack is eight centennial rooms, designed to celebrate 1776. These are based on historical fact with precise attention paid to the most minute detail.

Eugene Kupjack's antique shop depicted in the English Regency period.

Frederick Hicks's "Chinese Dining Room." Mr. Hicks sent the specifications to China and most of the parts were handcrafted there. The room, built in 1/12-inch scale, is 22 inches long, 12 inches high, and 19 inches deep. Wallpaper is from folio plates depicting the four seasons. A large window overlooks a rear garden; rattan screens shade the window, and the drapery hangings are black and gold. All parts, doors, drawers, etc., are movable, none are fixed or are parts permanently mounted. *Courtesy: Frederick Hicks and the Suffolk Museum at Stony Brook*

Also belonging to the more recent history of miniature setting and a maintainer of high standards for miniatures is Frederick Hicks. He developed 22 rooms from 1935 to 1942. (Wartime demands drew on Mr. Hicks's skills and he never was able to get back to miniature making.) These settings are now part of the collection of The Museums at Stony Brook, New York. Mr. Hicks constructed most of his own pieces as exact replicas of actual interiors. His precision is reflected even in the mortise and tenon construction of a cabinet drawer. Fixtures are workable. Things like drawer pulls are made with the help of a jeweler's lathe and carvings with dentist's burrs. Even his inlaid furniture is constructed with fruitwood veneers processed as in the life-size version.

With these excellent standards solidifying in the first half of the twentieth century, many exponents are maintaining these traditions. Their work graces the pages of this book.

One debate has emerged, however, and has not been resolved. If these rooms are to be seen and not used as a dollhouse, should construction exactly duplicate full-sized versions? Should drawers and doors open? Should mortise and tenon and other wood joint constructions be used? Paul Runyon, Harry Smith, Frederick Hicks, and others say "yes," that miniatures should be exactly formed down to the minutest detail whether visible or invisible. Others, such as Mrs. Thorne and Eugene Kupjack demonstrate that this is not necessary. What is important, according to the latter exponents, is that exterior visible details should be exacting. Since these miniature settings function only as displays

Frederick Hicks's Antique Shop contains over six hundred pieces of china, glass, porcelain, copper, pewter, brass, etc. It is a replica of an old barn showing pinned beams, feather-edge random paneling, a staircase and balcony in the rear, a fireplace and a large bay window on the left side with shelves. It is 27 1/2 inches long, 18 inches high, and 32 inches deep. *Courtesy: Frederick Hicks and the Suffolk Museum at Stony Brook*

A "1935 Modern" room by Frederick Hicks that contains a circular staircase, a fireplace, and mirror, handpainted wallpaper, two recessed cupboards, a large window on the right and a simulated black marble floor. *Courtesy: Frederick Hicks and the Suffolk Museum at Stony Brook*

that are not handled, objects are fixed in place and that is where they remain, in the settings, permanently. This same debate is going on between the authors of this book. Virginia Merrill does not believe construction has to duplicate full-sized versions, when used in environments. Creative improvisations in constructions take over. Thelma Newman, on the other hand, sees the construction of a miniature setting as a historical record that should be exact in every detail. How do you feel? The choice is yours. Both points of view will emerge as you read on.

We will see that there are three approaches to the "making" of miniature environments. Some aficionados collect and assemble pieces into settings, others create every detail themselves, but most people collect some elements from experts and make other pieces themselves. One does what is practical.

Decorating a room with precious "pure" miniature antiques or accurate facsimiles of styles and periods is a designing art. Collecting precise miniatures and combining them to scale in authentic environments is staging a setting, back in time, and can be a very challenging and dramatic experience. Imagine combining the plates and pots of Augustin Courtauld (an English prolific producer of dollhouse furnishings from 1708–1740) with furniture, ceramic jugs, glass bowls, pewter dishes, wall coverings, and flooring of that period. It can take a long time to assemble parts before there are enough pieces to furnish or inhabit a setting as though it were peopled. Let us look into putting parts together and setting some design standards for miniature settings in the next chapter. That is just a beginning. Later along in this book we'll describe how you can make your own miniature objects as well.

A collection of pieces that belong together on the way to creating an environment. The pieces were made by Harry Smith of Barnstable Originals. *Courtesy: Harry Smith, Barnstable Originals*

Another grouping of pieces made by Harry Smith, assembled before being combined with other similar period pieces into an environment. *Courtesy: Harry Smith, Barnstable Originals*

2 | PUTTING IT ALL TOGETHER

Putting all the parts together to create a miniature environment is really interior designing and stage designing rolled into one. It requires an equal mixture of good design, which some people call "good taste," and an understanding of the details and elements of a period or of a particular environment such as a library or florist shop.

Knowing the principles of color and design will help toward creating a significant and cohesive environment, and doing research will ensure that cultural indicators are accurately depicted. By proper annotation and measurements, the thinking, manners, and enthusiasms of each period will emerge, even in an unpeopled room. The end result, to be effective, has to exhibit a "personality" or have an "ambience," otherwise the product is mediocre. It may be that everything is correct from a theoretical point of view, but that extra "something" is missing—perhaps it is the use of color, texture, or lighting.

HOW TO BEGIN PLANNING

The principles of good interior design are the same whether the environment is furnished with period furnishings, with boxes and barrels, or in contemporary styles.

Decide what type of setting you are creating and what period in time it will depict. Do research. Look in books on antiques, at artists' paintings, in history books—wherever there are period indicators. Study the life-styles of the period. Look into seasonal differences of a setting and locations such as northern climates or southern areas. Take notes, sketch details, record measurements. After background study has been completed, you are ready to plan. Consider the following elements.

Respect architecture by treating windows, doorframes, size and shape of a setting with as much concern as the dovetail joinery in a cabinet drawer. *Consider large areas first.* Rugs, groups of curtained windows and wall areas form a background and help to unify separate elements. *Use only what is necessary* to complete the setting. Resist adding that extra glass vase because it belongs to the same period. Ask the question, "Does it belong or will the environment look better, less cluttered, without it?" *Consider the planes* created by heights of tables, cabinets, chairs, pictures. Try to limit the number of levels. One could end up with a ziggurat of heights that makes for a visual confusion. *Bring "natural" things* into a setting, those items that humanize, such as seasonal plants, knitting needles and yarn and a partially knitted

This vignette is a slice of an environment that looks as though it is inhabited. There is a sense of activity within the shallow depths of the frame. "The Gardener's Shed: Williamsburg" by Muriel Hoffman. *Courtesy: The Beehive Studio, Inc.*

A symmetrical setup with every element on wall and floor balanced equally on both sides of the imaginary fulcrum—in this case it is the candle on the table.

Two formal arrangements by Elizabeth Scull.

piece, wineglasses filled with wine, and so on. Most importantly, *use accessories that are perfect in scale and harmonize* with everything else. Consider proportion and take advantage of accessories to develop a focal point, or interest center, that will attract and hold one's attention. *Vary textures* with moderation, and keep patterns within limits —cabbage rose wallpaper, floral carpeting, different floral upholstery and drapery, flowers in vases, little things and doilies everywhere can be a horror to live with as well as to look at.

Planning

Floor planning is the beginning of room planning. This is the plan of what goes on the floor. Draw the shape of the environment (your box) on a piece of paper. If the room is to be a rectangle, then it should be translated into the shape of a trapezoid with slightly narrower measurements in the back and only the back plane and front parallel, or be set up at an angle to be more dynamic and visually interesting—attention getting and holding. This is because one should be viewing the completed setting at eye level. This is where designing for miniature interiors is closer to stage design than to interior design. Consider architectural features such as placement of doorways, fireplace, windows. Look into the activities that would go on in a setting—music, games, reading, writing, conversation, eating, watching TV. Consider, too, where lighting will be coming from to illuminate the areas of your setting. Will light shine in from windows, a skylight, storefront, candle flame, or lighting fixtures?

Indicate, in general, on your floor plan, where activities will take place. Then, on graph paper, to scale, sketch in contours of furniture arrangements. In a music area, for instance, you may have a piano, a light, a music storage cabinet, a piano stool or bench, a phonograph, and record storage cabinets. Keep traffic lanes in mind: how would people move through the area, as well as what will be seen or obscured as one looks into the setting. Do not consider this plan final. It should be an indicator, flexible in its intent.

Now sketch projections of walls. What will be seen against all three walls? And remember that everything does not sit up against a wall. Here, too, scale is important. When we talk of scale, we think of it in two senses: are the objects based consistently on one inch to the foot; and are furnishings in scale from a harmonious viewpoint? Are there too many massive pieces of furniture in too small an area? Is there a tiny picture placed over a long sofa, or a wide, tall lamp on a narrow table?

Consider your period. In the Middle Ages hardly any furniture was used by the common people. The wealthy lived in great halls with very large, high-ceiling rooms. Only massive furniture could make any impression on the otherwise stone or wood plank floors of these rooms. Until recently, there were few closets built into houses. Wardrobes, deep chests, and cabinets held all possessions. The wealthy lived in high-ceiling houses. The poor lived in houses with lower door openings and lower ceilings. Attention to details makes a difference.

Although this arrangement might appear to be asymmetrically balanced because the number of pieces are different on each side, the fulcrum is still on dead center with the imaginary visual weight equalized. (The fulcrum is to the left of the figure on the cabinet.) This kind of symmetrical balance tends to be less static than more formal arrangements. Needlepoint pillow, chairs, and all, made by Elizabeth Scull.

An arrangement showing informal or asymmetrical balance. The wing chair was made by Betty Valentine and the Queen Anne lowboy by Harry Smith.

Since Frederick Hicks's pieces are not fixed, they can be arranged in various ways. In this case they are lined up against the wall. If you look at each wall you will see that each area is symmetrical; hence the static look to the room. Note, however, that the proportion of rug to room size is perfect as are all the other appointments.

Allow for groupings of items and do use wallpaper to help tie parts together. Texture also helps to dramatize and emphasize. Repeats of verticals create a rhythm. "French Hat Shop" by Virginia Merrill.

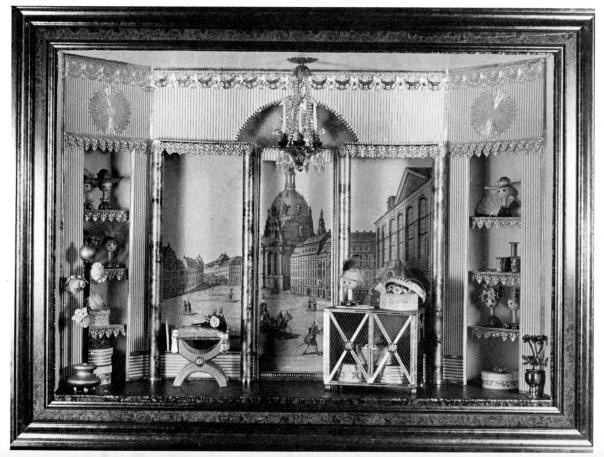

Look out for balance too. There should be a play of large furniture into units against smaller ones. Balance can be symmetrical or asymmetrical. In symmetrical balance, there is an equal distribution about a line, point, or plane of pairs or identical things such as a candlestick on each end of a mantelpiece, or a chair on each side of a table. Asymmetrical balance is balance where the fulcrum of the imaginary scale is not centered. Unmatched or unlike things are considered as bulk and can be "weighed" off against a blank space or a small grouping. The two candlesticks can be placed together at one end of the mantelpiece (the right side, for example) while a picture on the wall is hung slightly to the left.

If too much symmetrical balance is used, a room looks static and dull. The eye craves variety in size, color, and placement. In your final composition, balance of groups of furnishings is what is important. After at first considering the scale of single units, one becomes more conscious of shapes as they group into wholes or areas. Consider, too, that large areas such as wall panels, draperies, and rugs can affect balance as well as unify groups of furnishings in a setting or, more specifically, groups of furnishings within an area.

If you are having difficulty with the concept of balance, consider these techniques: *Balance with color and design* by placing something that seems weighty, such as two chairs covered with the same fabric, or a large picture grouped with a table and chair on the opposite side of the room from something that is heavy, such as a large sofa, cabinet, or a grand piano. *Avoid lonesome pieces* by not allowing a small piece to stand off by itself. Look for common planes or edges. Let lamp tables join (visually) edges of sofas and chairs. Place a floor lamp behind or beside a chair. *Balance with wall drama* by allowing a grouping of pictures, figured wallpaper, or patterned curtains to balance against a heavy piece of furniture on the opposite wall.

Color

At this point in planning, it is time to take an inventory of color—darks and lights, textures and patterns. These are very personal choices and also can make a great deal of difference in creating an atmosphere. Not only were certain color schemes more prevalent during certain periods, but colors also express all kinds of emotional content. Colors can be cold or warm, light and bright, or dark and gloomy. Color can stimulate or depress. Color effects change with seasons and times of the day. Color is dimension, inasmuch as it can make an area seem larger or smaller. Some colors tend to advance (reds and yellows), others tend to retreat (light blues, greens). Colors can mix or can clash. One decorator uses green sparingly when she wants to create a "green" room. Since blue and yellow are components of green, she uses grayed tones of blue and yellow on large background areas such as walls and carpeting. She also may use pure yellow for part of the upholstery and green only for accessories. Tints and shades of colors can "play" together to create rhythms in a room. Tints and shades which are light and dark values of a color can create illusions of size. Tints open up an area and tones tend to close in an area.

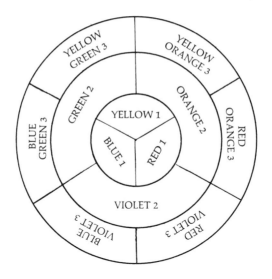

#1 PRIMARY COLORS — Yellow — Red — Blue
#2 SECONDARY COLORS — Green — Orange — Violet
#3 INTERMEDIATE COLORS — Yellow Green — Yellow Orange —
   Red Orange — Red Violet — Blue Violet — Blue Green

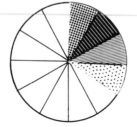

COMPLEMENTARY COLOR SCHEME
Opposite on Color Wheel

ADJACENT COLOR SCHEME
(Analogous)
Colors Are Side by Side

TRIAD COLOR SCHEME
The Use of Any 3 Colors which Divide
the Color Wheel into 3 Equal Parts

HUES — are bright colors
TONES — made by adding black to hues
TINTS — made by adding white to hues

The primary colors are basic hues and can be used together. Mixing any two primary colors together will create secondary colors. Blue and yellow make green; yellow and red produce orange; and mixing blue with red will result in purple. The varieties of each color can be enormous when we consider intensities and use of dark or light. Mixing colors with black will produce tones, and with white, tints. Opposite colors on the color wheel are complementary. When placed side by side they can vibrate or when tastefully combined in an environment they can enhance one another. The butcher uses green leaves next to red meat to make the meat look redder. Interestingly, a drop of a complementary color in its complement tends to gray down a color. Therefore, if a yellow is too bright, a drop of purple mixed into it will tone the yellow down to a grayer value so that the intensity is less harsh.

If you wish a restful, blending color scheme, use analogous colors on the color wheel, such as green, yellow-green and yellow, or blue, blue-green and green, and so on. If you wish more contrasting and dynamic effects, use a small amount of a complement in a setting where the other complement dominates. For instance, in a dominantly blue room, place some orange objects somewhere. Try different values—lights and darks of colors, the tints and tones with these color schemes.

How much of which color should be used? One of the most monotonous proportions, as you may know, is a one to one to one proportion or a one to two to three proportion. If all the walls are one color and all the furniture and maybe the curtains another color, and the rug still another color you may end up with a proportion of three to two to one, or a two to one to one proportion. These are too nearly equal to make for an interesting setting. Color areas should be more like one hundred to six to one for more drama. An accented scheme with a small area of a very sharp color claims your interest. For instance, there could be a green carpet, with the same color striped with white in curtains, yellow-green walls and both the greens in upholstery fabric; plus accent colors, such as coral red in a painting, in a collection of shells, in candles, on a pair of small chairs, or in pillows.

TEXTURE AND PATTERN

Texture is the quality of an object imparted to us basically by our sense of touch. But in the miniature, with textured proportions consid-

In this miniature Colonial American kitchen we find a rich use of texture. Textural elements repeat themselves as we look at the whole scene. Scale 1/2 inch to one foot. *Collection of Virginia Merrill.*

Although some of these pieces from the Tomorrow ® series of
April Day Collection would be excellent in a modern setting, as
an arrangement there is just too much of the same texture here.
Courtesy: The April Day Collections

This environment is rich in pattern and texture and looks too
cluttered. But that is deliberate and reflects well the over-fur-
nished Victorian room. *Collection of Eleanor McCown*

erably condensed, texture is revealed to us mainly by our sense of sight which translates or suggests the textural surface. In a way, texture is subtle pattern. Textures are suggested by the surface qualities of bricks, marble, wood, velvet, filmy silk, satin, the hard surface of bronze, glass, and so on. Pattern is more obvious. It puts a leash on the eye by leading vision step by step through an arrangement of lines, shapes, or areas of color or shade on a given surface. A checkerboard is a pattern, books on a shelf are patterns, so are folds of a drapery, grillwork, latticework, a bull's-eye, the arrangement of fruit in a bowl.

A boldly striped curtain may direct your attention to the plush texture on the rug below. A pattern of widely spaced lattices can lead you off beyond confines of the room into some distant space. Pattern and texture can make a room look larger or smaller. Use of too many patterns can create an animated effect, psychologically closing in the space. Light-colored smooth and soft textures in an almost monochromatic color scheme appear to open up a space. Up-and-down stripes on a wallpaper, in an illusory way, makes a room appear higher; and conversely, horizontally striped paper can "bring a ceiling down."

MORE ON DESIGNING A SETTING

Every three-dimensional setting consists of a combination of lines—vertical, horizontal, diagonal, curving, crossing, pointing. They psychologically imply emotional qualities. Lines in an environment can suggest repose, conflict, majesty, strength, weakness. Straight vertical lines intimate majesty and strength—the majesty of a Gothic cathedral,

Rich in line and texture and full of rhythm, placement of objects leads the eye to the center of interest (dramatized by diagonals). One would expect a person to walk through those swinging doors. "The Saloon" circa 1895 was made by Iova Vaughn. *Courtesy: The Beehive Studio, Inc.*

the majesty and strength of a forest of redwood. Horizontal lines indicate repose, relaxation, such as a bed, couch, long low cocktail table, and long low cabinets. The diagonal line is one of action. It is dynamic and suggests speed. Some curves and spirals appear even more active than the diagonal.

In designing a setting, one can take advantage of line by allowing for a predominance of certain lines; a particular effect can be created as indicated above. But, importantly, line denotes a sense of order. And line can suggest rhythm. By repeating lines, rhythms are created that can transport a dull setting into a striking one. Rhythm is manifested through repeats of curves, from folds of drapes or curtains, from architectural elements such as windows, and from details such as pictures and pillows and panels. Since pictures and pillows especially are color-bearers, colors can produce rhythm as they echo and repeat in different parts of a room. Rhythm in a room design can be elusive and difficult to achieve. It is sometimes intangible, but the room's glory depends on it.

THE PLACE OF CARPETS, WINDOW AND WALL COVERINGS

Floor covering represents a major color and design influence in a room. When considering whether to use a carpet or rugs, or whether to keep a floor bare, consider the period, function of the room, and color. Keep figured carpets and rugs very quiet in design if there are many outstanding patterns in the room. If there are fine paintings on the wall for instance, or prominently figured wallpaper, plain or textured rugs or carpets look best. You might look into a sculptured Chinese carpet effect.

Floor coverings should fit a room. Size is important. A small room should have a margin of bare floor around the carpet of no more than one-half inch. (That measurement is translated from six inches of actual size.) A large room can afford a margin of bare floor of about one inch to one and one-half inches. Furniture should fit comfortably on

Although the chandelier halfway obliterates one's view of the dominant painting on the wall, the main carpet is plain and noncompeting. A smaller area rug in front of the fireplace helps to tie together the two seating arrangements on either side of the fireplace. *Furnishings in this living room were made by Eric Pearson. Collection of Mrs. John Coward*

the carpet, unless the furniture backs up to a wall. A skimpy island of a carpet can give the room a "restless" appearance.

Area rugs should be used when flooring detail is outstanding, or when the room is large and divided into several centers.

Curtains and draperies frame a view, create an effect of privacy and insulation, unify a series of windows, and act as a backdrop for sitting areas or groupings of furniture.

If windows appear to be too far apart after you have constructed your setting, overall treatment of curtains and draperies across the wall and windows helps to unify or tie together the disparate feelings of the widely spaced windows.

Wall treatments can vary from fireplaces to woodwork, pictures and ornaments, radiators, wall coverings. Styles of a period will dictate what the fashion should be in your creation. A great deal of drama can occur by using wall covering treatments such as textiles in panels, wood paneling, patterned or figured wallpaper, organization of paintings, mirrors, lighting fixtures, and carefully considering how all of this is combined. Don't fix these accessory parts permanently until you experiment a bit with combinations and are satisfied.

LIGHTING EFFECTS

Is your setting going to exist in a daylight setting, evening, or during what season? The color of light will affect colors in your room and certainly plays a large part in creating a mood.

Lighting effects play an important part in the drama of a setting as seen in the two versions of this French sidewalk café from the collection of Susan Richardson. *By Eugene Kupjack.*

Willoughby's hexagonal "Lanthorn" House (from the collection of Virginia Merrill) certainly looks more dramatic when lighted.

Are you to include chandeliers, wall sconces, table or floor lamps? Is light to come in through the window for daylight effects or be derived solely from lamps or candles?

Rooms that are to present a nighttime effect should be several shades darker in value than a daytime setting. A greenhouse, for example, should be bright and light, compared to a study or library. Color plays along with light effects. They are actually inseparable and integrated. Consider light as a tool and as a function of the architecture. You have to plan for it early in your set designing.

More about setting up lighting effects later.

ROOM STYLES AND THEIR COMPONENTS

Although it is not absolutely necessary, many miniaturists allow one furniture style to predominate in a setting. This is not always natural because good quality furnishings, in the full-scale environment, often have been inherited and otherwise accumulated over the years with several styles attractively presiding in the same room. As a historical record, it probably is best to keep the same period styles together. But there is no hard-and-fast rule that can be applied here. Taste will govern choice. Here are some examples of elements that belong together for design consistency.

For an Early American room, this is what to look for:

>   solid woods, simply stained and waxed, particularly pine and maple
>   simple brass hardware
>   splat-back chairs, wing chairs, double chair settees
>   high and low chests
>   simple paneled doors
>   classical wood-trimmed fireplaces
>   colorful cotton fabrics
>   pewter, china, and glass accessories
>   hooked and rag braided rugs with patterns or small allover designs

For an eighteenth-century room, this is what to look for:

>   dark woods with fine furnishings
>   intricate carvings such as acanthus leaf and honeysuckle, ram's head, winged griffin and lion, laurel, garland and urn
>   high and low cabinets
>   paintings
>   paneled walls with moldings and trims, often coverings within panels of rich fabrics
>   silks, damasks, brocades
>   fine china and silver accessories
>   room-sized rugs and area carpets in rich colors and pastels
>   small patterns or quiet allover patterns

For a contemporary room, this is what to look for:

>   straight architectural lines devoid of trims but use of rich textures such as brick or wood-paneled walls
>   broad expanse of glass
>   various woods
>   simple, functional furniture design
>   flush rather than paneled doors
>   low bookcases, cabinets, and tables
>   sculpture, prints, and paintings
>   functional accessories of wood, glass, ceramic, metal, and plastics
>   textured fabrics, simple, geometric patterns
>   plain and textured carpets—wall to wall or area rugs

Within these broad categories are many styles of furnishings. These style differences fluctuated in prominence depending on time and place. Some periods are highlighted by styles of famous furniture makers. The Adam period is one. The Adam brothers' designs dominated the English scene for fifty years. Other periods were named after a movement, such as the Empire period, a location such as Windsor after

Windsor Castle, or a famous person such as Victorian after Queen Victoria.

In this chapter you will find a chart, complete with diagrams of typical furniture, that helps to organize and somewhat simplifies categories.

SOME FURNITURE STYLES AND THEIR PERIODS

All of the following are miniature furniture.

Walnut bombé storage cabinet—17th-century Dutch, 1/12-inch scale, made by Paul A. Runyon. Collection of Virginia Merrill.

William and Mary arched top highboy. Walnut was the predominant wood used in furniture during this period, 1688–1702. A second-size piece in the collection of Jeanne Knoop.

A second-size Queen Anne period bureau desk in walnut with inlay. Chairs, china cupboards, and secretary-desks were made of walnut during this period, 1702–1714. Collection of Jeanne Knoop.

A Queen Anne highboy by Donald C. Buttfield in 1/12-inch scale, along with a full-sized finial.

The large Queen Anne period lowboy is an antique made of cherry wood. The duplicate, in miniature, is a second-size reproduction made by S. A. Raube.

A Queen Anne settee and piecrust tilt-top table. Both made by Willoughby's.

Transitional (post) Queen Anne knife box, tea table, and armchair, all made in second size by S. A. Raube.

The Windsor chair originated at Windsor Castle in England early in the 18th century. Bentwood back frame varied to comb-back. The splayed legs pegged directly into the seat and the seat was often thick and saddle-shaped. It was a favorite chair of the American colonists. This one, and spice cabinet of about the same period, is in 1/12th-inch scale and made by Donald C. Buttfield.

Chippendale style furniture was originally designed or influenced by Thomas Chippendale (1718–1779), an English cabinetmaker. His work dominated the mid-18th century in England. This 1/4-size Chippendale style desk is of mahogany and made by Paul A. Runyon.

A Chippendale style second-size-chair made by S. A. Raube.

A Chippendale style mahogany settee made by Eric Pearson. Styles of furniture in England were often classified by the predominant wood used. The Age of Oak was 1500–1660, the Age of Walnut was from 1660–1720, the Age of Mahogany was 1720–1765, and the Age of Satinwood 1765–1800.

A Chippendale style four-poster bed in mahogany in 1/12th-inch scale made by Paul A. Runyon.

A Chinese Chippendale china cabinet. Chinese motifs were adopted to ornament 18th-century English furniture. Chippendale himself used many of these designs. Made by Virginia Merrill.

Here we jump the Atlantic Ocean to Colonial America and Shaker style furniture. This is a bake table.
Courtesy: Philip Wilson Handcrafted Miniatures

This is a Shaker fireside chair. Shaker furniture was functional in design with the same piece used for many purposes. *Courtesy: Philip Wilson Handcrafted Miniatures*

An Old Barrack's spinning wheel of beefwood of mid-18th-century style. Made by Paul A. Runyon. *Collection of Ruth Runyon.*

Hepplewhite furniture, after the style of George Hepplewhite, who worked with the Adam brothers, was produced with simple classical lines in the late 18th century. This working tall case clock is in the Hepplewhite style, made in mahogany with inlay by Paul A. Runyon.

A Carver chair Centennial piece, mid-18th century, in second size. *Collection of Jeanne Knoop.*

A Hepplewhite style chest in mahogany by Paul A. Runyon.

A late 18th-century American tilt-top table in mahogany. It is 4 1/2 inches high with a table diameter of 5 inches. *Courtesy: Philadelphia Museum of Art Bequest of Henrietta Morris Bonsal*

A Pennsylvania "wagon" seat circa 19th century made in second size by Dr. Charles L. Stone.

Victorian style furniture predominated (1837–1901) in both England and America during the time of Queen Victoria. Greek and Gothic motifs were lavishly mixed with Turkish, Venetian, Egyptian, and Louis XV influences. Plush upholstered furniture was very popular. These Victorian pieces were made by Elizabeth Scull.

A Victorian style sewing table inlayed with mother-of-pearl by Virginia Merrill.

A Victorian bedroom suite from the Miniature Mart. *Courtesy: The Miniature Mart*

Ice-cream chairs were popular during the early and mid-
20th century—and for that matter, to this day. *Courtesy:*
Philip Wilson Handcrafted Miniatures

A contemporary solid redwood glider and garden chair.
Courtesy: Philip Wilson Handcrafted Miniatures

Contemporary hand-carved 1/8th scale black walnut furniture by Jocko Johnson. *Courtesy: Jocko Johnson*

Acrylic contemporary furniture from the "Tomorrow" series by April Day Creations. *Courtesy: April Day Creations*

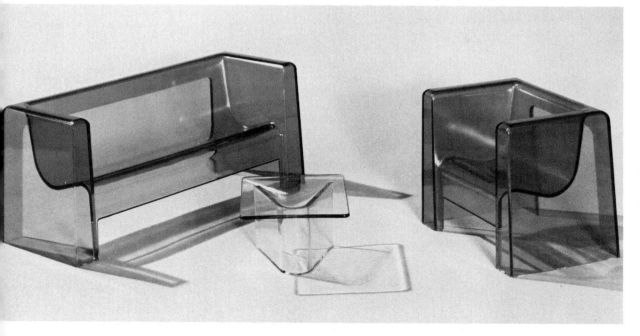

Rooms housed in a cabinet, in effect a dollhouse, were among the earliest collections of miniatures. Collection: Mrs. John McCown.

Miniature chandelier made of beads, jewelry findings, and wax-dipped toothpicks. From the Peddlers Shop.

Sterling silver miniature coffee services executed in the lost-wax process.

Petit point rug by Jean Jessop.

Chippendale secretary by Paul A. Runyon, one inch to the foot, is an exact duplicate of a full-scale version.

Contemporary room with "stained glass" window, formed acrylic furniture, and carpeted conversational pit. By Thelma R. Newman.

Bouquet of roses made from epoxy putty and vase turned from a spool. By Virginia Merrill.

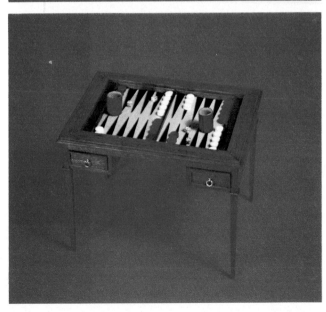

Backgammon table with marquetry. Backgammon pieces made by slicing knitting needles. Top 3½" X 2¼". By Donald C. Buttfield.

A crib by Andrew and Susan Grainger, 4½ inches tall.

Miniature overshot weaving in a bedspread by Lillian A. Gaines.

Upholstered Victorian parlor set by Virginia Merrill.

Sitting room, Queen Anne period by Eugene Kupjack.

Miniature tapestry designed and made by Jean Jessop.
5" X 3".

Circle of potted plants enamel over bronze from Austria.
The entire display is 5" tall.

Federal period panel screen in decoupage design.
By Virginia Merrill.

Victorian pastry table. Foods made of ceramic, clay, and epoxy. By Virginia Merrill.

Black lacquer secretary with raised gold leaf chinoiserie design by Virginia Merrill. 7" high by 4" wide.

Romanian peasant's cottage interior.

Miniature scene that sits on a table, an antique hat shop under a glass dome by Mary Jones.

Tinsel painting by Mariette Paine Slayton. 2" X 2½". Collection: Janet Gales.

Upholstered chair by Dolphin Originals, table by Paul A. Runyon, painting by Mariette Paine Slayton. Scale is shown by the cigarette.

Miniature room that fits on a bookshelf by Eugene Kupjack.

A general store by Perry Fisher.

SOME ROOM STYLES OF DIFFERENT PERIODS

These are all miniature settings.

English, late Tudor period (1550–1600) during the reign of Elizabeth, 1558–1603. The hall was a common living room and reception room of the manor house. Characteristics were paneled-back benches, "wainscot" chairs, and "melon bulb" turnings on tables and cupboards. This setting was created by Frederick Hicks. *Courtesy: Frederick Hicks*

Dutch influence was apparent in Queen Anne period rooms. Oriental fabrics were used, cabriole legs and bureau style desks appeared. Chair backs showed new attention to comfort. These furnishings and interior by Eugene Kupjack.

Chinese Chippendale and Thomas Chippendale-influenced furniture predominate in this room that could have existed in England between 1760–1775, except for the lamp. Candles would have been used in a chandelier in this kind of setting. Made by Frederick Hicks. *Courtesy: Frederick Hicks*

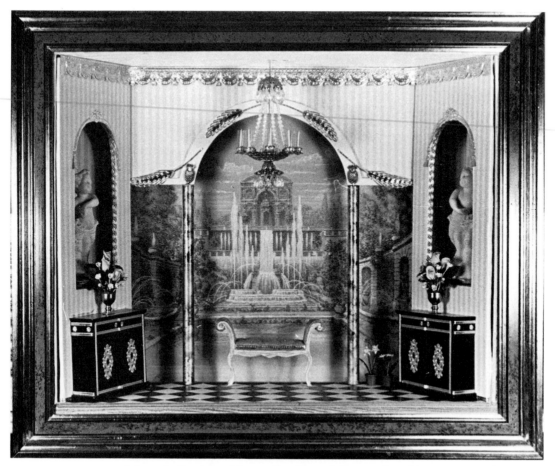

A foyer in the style of the pre-Empire period, somewhere between 1793 and 1804. Classic motifs were taken from ancient vases and frescoes. Frescoes in the style of Pompeii were popular with floral, pastoral, and garden motifs. Reds, yellows, golds, and black became dominant. Marble and mosaics appeared as floor coverings. Ebony and light fruitwoods shared the setting with a liberal use of gilded finishes. This foyer was made by Virginia Merrill.

A French Normandy bedroom and boudoir of the 18th century. Ceilings were beamed, doors and cabinets were paneled and textiles repeated the pattern of wall coverings. Wing chairs were used near fireplaces to keep off drafts. Setting and furnishings by Eugene Kupjack.

A Colonial American setting somewhere around late 17th to early 18th century. Floor coverings used were braided and hooked rugs. Wicker and caning were employed on chairs. Benches with high backs served to keep out drafts. Leaded windows, opening outward, were common in Massachusetts, particularly. Furnishings and setting by Frederick Hicks. *Courtesy: Frederick Hicks*

A New Hampshire Shaker type of sewing room, early 19th century. *Collection of Eleanor McCown*

Federal period hallway. Classical furniture appeared mid- and late 18th century in the early days of the Republic. Adam, Hepplewhite, Sheraton, and Regency influences came from England; Louis XIV, Directoire, and Empire influences from France; and Duncan Phyfe was an important designer. *Collection of Eleanor McCown*

This bedroom could have existed in a Virginia home the mid- to late 18th century. Chippendale influences in furniture were popular. Furnishings and setting by Frederick Hicks. *Courtesy: Frederick Hicks*

A late-18th-century American working kitchen. *Courtesy: Metropolitan Museum of Art, The Sylmaris Collection*

A 20th-century-style living room, eclectic in design, inasmuch as it draws upon furniture of many periods. Furnishings and setting by Frederick Hicks. *Courtesy: Frederick Hicks*

A vignette of a contemporary Mexican shop. Mexican pottery, baskets, and weavings predominate. Made by Laura Davis. *Courtesy: The Beehive Studio, Inc.*

An early-20th-century bathroom. *Courtesy: Mary Jane Graham of It's A Small World*

"1935 modern" living room with hand-painted wallpaper, mirrored fireplace wall, and venetian blinds. By Frederick Hicks. *Courtesy: Frederick Hicks*

A contemporary room designed by George Nelson & Company in 1/12th-inch scale. Columns were made from groupings of basswood T sections. The dome was vacuum-formed from polystyrene sheet. The grill, below the dome, was constructed from a honeycomb material. Carpeting was made of toweling. The stool in the extreme right was a drawer pull with a small cushion put on the "screw" part. Actual drawer pulls were improvised of pin heads. The sculptures on the central tables came from charm bracelets. *Courtesy: George Nelson & Company*

BEGINNING YOUR SETTING—CONSTRUCTING A BASIC BOX

Most settings start with a box or some kind of container. Boxes can be easily transported, assembled, and displayed. Other settings are installed in cabinets, niches, on shelves and, more rarely, in lamps and other accessories. (Chapter 3 covers a range of possibilities.) In putting together an environment one always works from the general to the particular.

Before a basic box is constructed, a plan will have been drawn and most materials assembled. All research with annotations and measurements has to be gathered.

The exterior of the box is then constructed with hinged sides and/or backs where one needs access to lighting. It is best to plan wall angles so that they are not straight, dull walls but more like a stage set which psychologically draws you into the setting by the use of dynamic wall angles.

After the walls have been planned, the flooring goes in *first.* If the walls are at an angle, then floorboards and tiles have to be consistently angled as well. If the floor is made of wood, it has to be stained.

Next the walls are built. One could play around with wall arrangements before permanently gluing them (with a white glue), and reinforcing them with blocks of wood. Before anchoring the walls, however, they should be trimmed with moldings, painted, paneled, or otherwise decorated with wall coverings.

Next, stairways and banisters are built. After that, doors are cut and hinged into place but they are constructed to be stationary. The ceiling is then painted and placed over the top of the walls. Gluing the ceiling into place can wait or be attached at this point.

Windows are made complete with panes, curtains, and draperies attached, before fastening all these units into place. After everything is affixed, lighting is installed through the openings in the sides and back of the box. Lamps, chandeliers, window lighting effects, fireplace flicker flames, candle flames—all are connected to the electrical system.

Carpeting and rugs are then placed on the floor, often tacked by pegging furniture legs (two or four) through the carpeting into the floor, to keep furniture and floor covering from moving or shifting.

After larger pieces of furnishings are in place, books are glued on shelves, and accessories such as ceramics are anchored, often with florist's clay. The smallest accessory details are last to be inserted.

A basic room ready to receive furnishings by Donald C. Buttfield.

When all parts have been assembled, the exterior of the box is papered or painted and a frame containing glass is attached to the front. This frame should be removable. You can use either hooks and eyes or hinges and latches.

When everything has been assembled, the completed setting should be jar-proof and travel-proof.

A ready-made shell of a room by Philip Wilson of Handcrafted Miniatures. *Courtesy: Philip Wilson Handcrafted Miniatures*

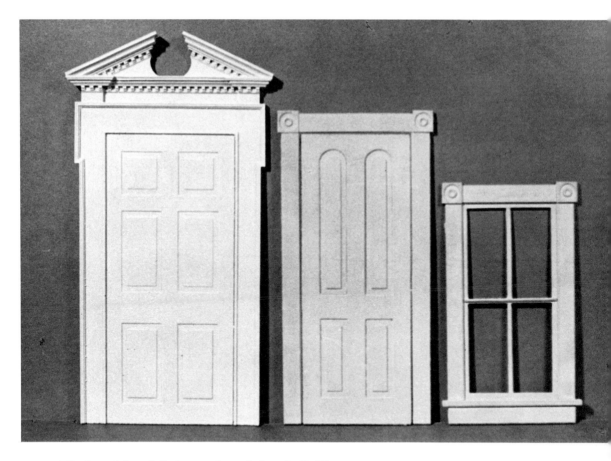

Wood appointments that are ready-made from the Peddlers
Shop. *Courtesy: The Peddlers Shop*

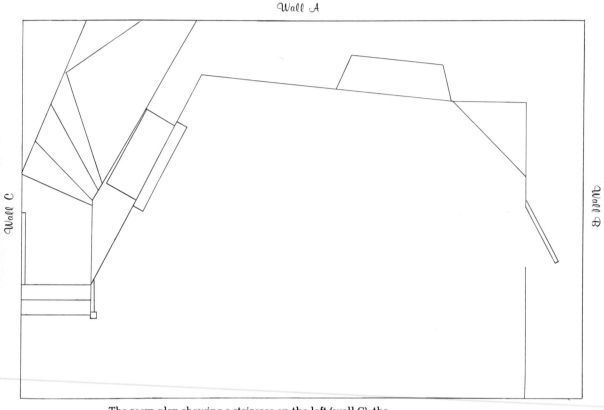

The room plan showing a staircase on the left (wall C), the fireplace angled on the left, a bay window on wall A and a corner cabinet in corner A-B, and a door opening on wall B.

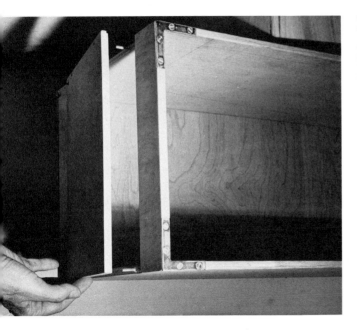

The basic box is constructed of birch-faced plywood allowing for an opening where one can have access later to the lighting fixtures. Note the angle reinforcements on the front opening.

The side and back openings are attached with bolts and wing nuts.

The first interior modifications begin. We are looking at wall A and the start of the construction of the bay window. At about the same time the flooring is put into place using strips of basswood. Three coats of antique cherry stain are used and then the whole floor is varnished four or five times, sanding between coats.

 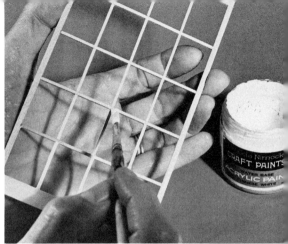

Strips of basswood for the window frame are cut and then adjusted to size with an X-Acto knife. Parts are attached with Elmer's Glue. (A toothpick is used to clean off excess glue.)

The completed window frame is painted with white acrylic paint using a camelhair brush.

The thinnest windowpane glass is used with the frame glued to the glass to help keep the frame from warping. Clear acrylic sheet, 1/16th inch, can be used as well, so can cellulose acetate.

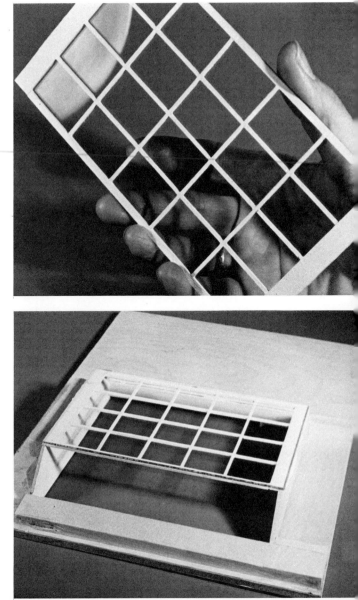

The frame is attached with white glue to the bay window construction.

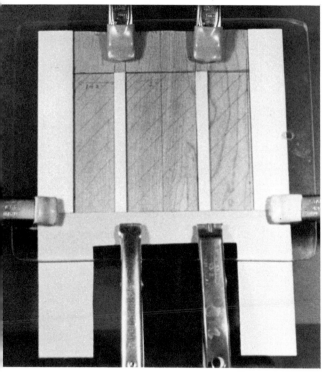

Next the panel wall for around the fireplace is cut to shape from a thin sheet of basswood (1/16th-inch) with superimposed panel pieces glued in place using white glue. Note that a piece of clear acrylic is overlayed so clamps hold the newly glued pieces in place (without marring the surface) until the glue dries. One also can see through the acrylic whether there has been any shifting of the overlayed panel pieces.

The brickwork for the fireplace interior is made by scoring the basswood shape with a triangular jeweler's file. A steel ruler guides the file. The surface is roughened slightly with course sandpaper to imitate brick surfaces.

The completed paneled fireplace wall painted white using acrylic paint.

Then, fireplace bricks are painted a mottled brick red with acrylic imitating the brick color and texture. Then the "bricks" are glued into place.

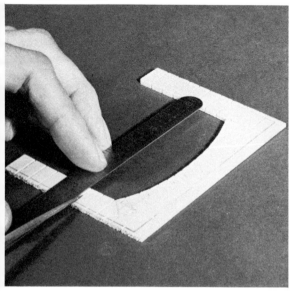

The stairway construction for Wall C is shown here glued and painted.

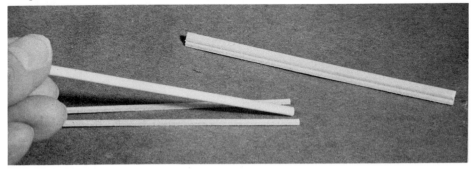

Banisters for the stairway are cut from strips of basswood using two flat pieces and one round strip. Some pieces are turned on a jeweler's lathe.

Wall C is paneled and painted. Then the stairway wall is papered with a toile paper executed in a silk screen process. The stairway is inserted and the fireplace wall is fixed in place. Sometimes steel right-angle reinforcements are screwed into the back behind the scene.

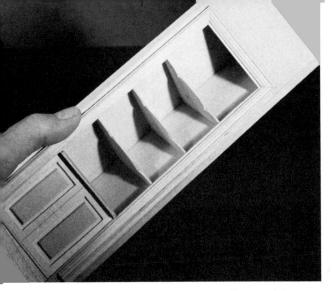

The corner cabinet between Walls A and B is constructed of basswood and then painted white.

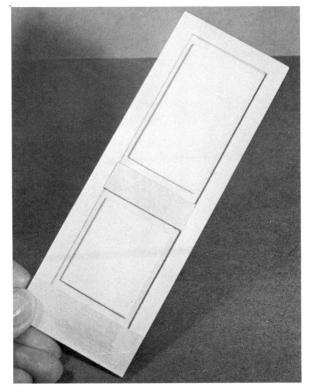

Doors are made of 1/16-inch basswood as a base and then 1/16-inch panel strips are glued in place. Sometimes edges are carved to simulate moldings. Any spaces between joints are filled; the doors are painted and hardware is attached.

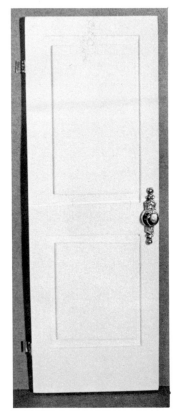

A paneled dado is added. The window seat is upholstered and drapery is formed flat (see Chapter 5 for the process) and then fixed in place with glue (from the front) and, if needed, nailed from the back.

Banisters, ceiling molding, corner cabinet, and doors are now in place. Next comes wiring for lighting—the candlesticks on the fireplace wall, the flicker light for the fireplace, and lighting for the bay window and hallway door are attached and wired to a transformer.

A back view of Wall A showing lighting fixtures and wiring.

A view from the back opening of Wall B showing the transformer hookup. (More on basic lighting follows.)

Furnishings are made, or acquired, and fixed permanently into place. Even the out-of-window scene can be viewed. Some of the processes of making parts are shown farther along in the book. The completed room, modeled after an original by Eugene Kupjack.

LIGHTING: WAYS, MEANS, AND MATERIALS*

Some well-qualified miniaturists maintain that, since light cannot be scaled down, lighting fixtures or bulbs should not be used inside the miniature room. Leaving obvious arguments aside, we will agree that, given the proper room and a large enough box, simulated sunlight streaming through the doors and windows of a miniature room does provide a very realistic effect. An ordinary lightbulb, located outside the windows, has been used very effectively for the Thorne rooms which are on display in the Chicago Art Institute and in rooms executed by Kupjack and by Carlson. To obtain the proper effect in any room lighted in this manner, the size and location of the door and/or window through which the simulated sunlight is to enter must be chosen with care. The bulb, too, must be of the proper size, and located in such a manner as to create the best effects of lights and shadows. Generally speaking, this technique is not suitable for the more popular small boxes which measure less than fifteen inches wide.

Before installing lights or bulbs in a miniature room, one must consider the purpose of lighting the room. A miniature room is usually lighted for one of three reasons: first to facilitate viewing the miniature objects and interior detail; second, to simulate outdoor lighting on a scene which is outside a door or window of the room, or third, to animate the room and provide thorough realism. If the purpose of the lighting is to improve viewing of the interior detail, one very simple and effective technique involves the use of a 115-volt, 7-watt bulb. This type of bulb is commonly used for night-lights and pilot lights and is obtainable at most hardware stores, together with the required socket. For this method, the room is equipped with a false ceiling, of frosted glass, located about one and a half inches below the top of the box. The 115-volt bulb is installed between this ceiling and the top of the box. Use of a yellow bulb above such a ceiling is especially effective for rustic or old-fashioned settings, as it imparts a subdued light much like candlelight. The bulb socket is spliced directly to a line cord which, in turn, plugs directly into the wall socket of your home. Although the 7-watt bulb is relatively small, it does generate a significant amount of heat. For this reason, ventilation should be provided by drilling three or four small holes in the back of the box at a point above the glass ceiling and near the top of the box. Extreme caution must be used when wiring a miniature room with a 115-volt bulb. This much voltage is dangerous and, under certain circumstances, can be lethal. Any splices made in 115-volt wires *must* be soldered and *must* be insulated by wrapping properly with vinyl plastic electrical tape.

A better system for providing general lighting for a miniature room utilizes a safe, low voltage derived from a transformer to light several small bulbs which may be hidden on the ceiling or behind the frame of the box. When properly executed, this system provides a more evenly distributed light than does the 115-volt bulb. Small, fluorescent-type bulbs, called "fluorettes," which measure about 1 1/2 inches long

*Special thanks goes to Ed Leonard of Illinois Hobbycraft for writing this section.

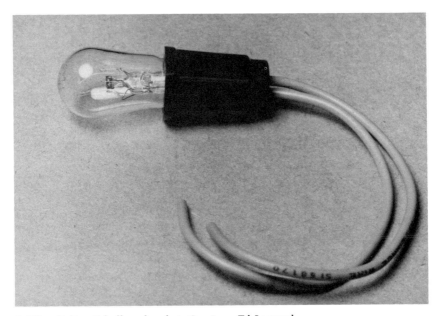

A 115-volt, 7-watt bulb and socket. *Courtesy: Ed Leonard*

and 1/4 inch in diameter, are especially suitable for this lighting method. These tiny, tubular bulbs operate from a 12-volt transformer and offer the advantage of being easily replaced when they burn out.

Many miniature rooms feature an outdoor scene which is located behind a false wall and is visible through a window or door in the room. Because the area behind the false wall is exceptionally dark, it is almost always desirable to illuminate such a scene. In real life, the entire outdoor scene would be evenly lighted by the sun. The miniaturist must keep this in mind when planning the lighting. If the scene is viewed through a single door or window, one bulb of adequate size will provide sufficient illumination. For this case the single 115-volt, 7-watt bulb may be used and the same precautions taken as described above. If the scene is viewed through an exceptionally large window or through two openings, it may be better to provide more than one bulb in order to distribute the lighting evenly. Two or more of the small, 12-volt fluorettes mentioned earlier will provide even lighting to a back wall scene.

Miniature electric lights and fixtures, when incorporated into the room itself, seem to animate the scene and add a new dimension of interest. There are a number of accurately scaled lighting fixtures suitable for this purpose. In addition, there are many fixtures which can be equipped with tiny lightbulbs and made to operate. In every case, the lighting of miniature fixtures or lamps requires the use of very small bulbs which operate from some voltage lower than the 115 volts obtained from your wall socket.

Regardless of the number or types of bulbs used, the basic techniques for wiring a miniature room are much the same. The primary components required are: a power source such as a transformer or battery, wire, and the lights or bulbs. If a transformer is used, a line cord will also be required. The relationship of these components is shown in the schematic diagram.

Batteries may be used for lighting a miniature room if there is to be only a single bulb or miniature lamp lighted. If two or more bulbs are lighted from a battery, the life of the battery is shortened to such an extent that its use is not economical. If batteries are to be used, the C size flashlight cell is preferred because these cells provide a reasonably long life while occupying a relatively small space. Experience indicates that alkaline cells will last about four times longer than carbon-zinc cells.

The transformer required to power the average miniature room lighting system need be no larger than two C cells and, in fact, may be much smaller. While the initial cost of a transformer may be higher than that of the equivalent battery and battery holder, the cost is repaid many times in savings realized from not replacing batteries. A transformer is a device which reduces the 115 volts obtained from the wall outlet of your home to some lower, safer voltage. It has no moving parts and, if properly used, will never wear out. Transformers are rated according to the voltage they deliver after the 115 volts has been reduced. For miniature room lighting, a transformer rated at 12 volts is most desirable. To assure long life for the miniature bulbs, the transformer output must be stable and must not be higher than the voltage rating of the bulbs to be used. Many transformers deliver voltages

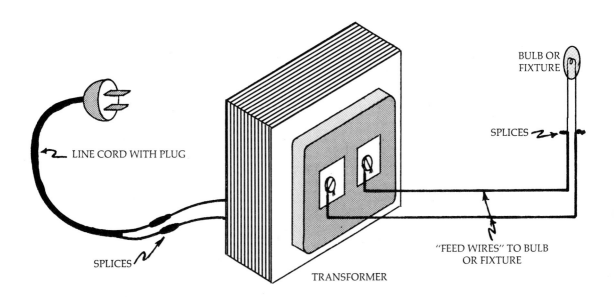

BULB OR FIXTURE

SPLICES

LINE CORD WITH PLUG

"FEED WIRES" TO BULB OR FIXTURE

SPLICES

TRANSFORMER

SCHEMATIC DIAGRAM
SINGLE BULB OR FIXTURE CONNECTED TO TRANSFORMER

The schematic diagram shows the complete wiring arrangement for a miniature room which is to be lighted with a single bulb or light. If two or more lights are to be used, the additional units are also connected directly to the transformer. *Courtesy: Ed Leonard*

which vary widely, according to the number of bulbs connected. Such transformers, although rated at 12 volts, may actually deliver as much as 16 volts when only a single miniature bulb is connected. Use of such a transformer will seriously shorten the life of the bulbs when only one bulb or a few are connected. Toy train transformers and miniature race car transformers, because of their design factors, deliver an especially high voltage when used to light one or two small bulbs and therefore should never be used for miniature room lighting. Some dollhouse and miniature shops offer a complete line of miniature lighting equipment which includes several sizes of 12-volt transformers suitable for small, medium, and large lighting systems. If possible, it is best to use a transformer that has been selected for its stable voltage output and known performance characteristics. If a miniature lighting transformer cannot be obtained, a 10-volt doorbell or chime transformer, available at most hardware stores, is very suitable for miniature lighting. Although rated at 10 volts, these transformers actually deliver between 12 and 14 volts, depending upon the number of bulbs connected. Most doorbell/chime transformers will supply enough electricity to light about eight grain-of-wheat bulbs or four of the larger screw base (flashlight type) bulbs.

A line cord, obtainable at hardware stores, connects the transformer to the 115-volt wall outlet. The easiest ones to use are made of vinyl plastic and have a plug molded onto one end. If a vinyl plastic line cord is not obtainable, buy a vinyl plastic extension cord and cut off the socket end, not the plug!

The wire used for feeding electricity to the miniature lights and fixtures in a miniature room, the "feed wire," must be of the smallest diameter practical to effect concealment of the wires and not interfere with a realistic appearance. Wire sizes are indicated by "gauge numbers." Oddly enough, the larger the gauge number, the smaller the wire size will be. Thirty-two gauge insulated wire, which measures less than 1/32 inch in diameter, is the smallest size commonly available. This wire can be found in some miniature and dollhouse shops that offer lighting system equipment but is not easily found in ordinary retail stores. Vinyl insulated wire of 28, 30, or 32 gauge is recommended for miniature wiring because the vinyl jacket permits easy removal of the insulation, and its small size makes concealment easy. This wire may be obtained in colors such as white, black, and brown to match the woodwork of your miniature room. Hobby shops that specialize in model railroad equipment often stock a very small size wire which is used for internal wiring of model locomotives and cars. Telephone and communication companies use 24- and 26-gauge wire to connect their equipment. While these wire sizes are comparatively large, they may be used for miniature wiring, and the scrap end from a single cable will provide enough wire for dozens of miniature rooms.

Bulbs used to light a miniature room may be the screw-base type (similar to a flashlight bulb) which screws into a tiny socket or the grain-of-wheat type which requires no socket. This latter type bulb is equipped with lead wires about six inches long which are used to

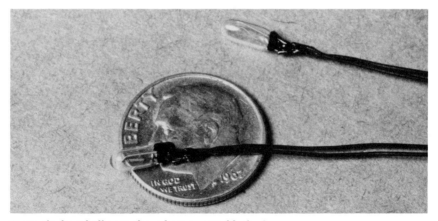

Grain-of-wheat bulbs are the only type suitable for lamps
and fixtures because of being accurately scaled. *Courtesy:*
Ed Leonard

connect it to the source of electricity. Because of its very small size, the
grain-of-wheat bulb is the only type suitable for applications where
accurately scaled lamps and fixtures are desired. The bulbs used in a
12-volt lighting system may be rated at either 12 or 16 volts. If ordinary
12-volt bulbs are used, they will have a normal life expectancy. This
means that they may last a few months or a year before they burn out.
If 16-volt bulbs are used, the 4-volt difference in their rating provides
a cushion that absorbs voltage fluctuations or variations in transformer
output, and thereby extends the life of the bulb. When 16-volt bulbs are
used with a 12-volt transformer, their life will be as much as five times
that of an ordinary 12-volt bulb used with the same transformer. Some
miniature lighting suppliers offer a special 12-volt "long-life" grain-of-
wheat bulb with a life expectancy of 10,000 or more hours. This is
equivalent to about seven years of service if the bulbs are turned on for
four hours every day. Because grain-of-wheat bulbs are not easily replaced, either the 16-volt or 12-volt long-life type should be used with
a 12-volt transformer to assure maximum operating life.

Planning for the installation of lighting should begin before construction of the miniature room is started. If a false wall is to be used,
it is best to make the back of the box removable to facilitate installation
of electrical equipment and wiring. The transformer hiding place can
often be made a part of the room construction. Transformers as small
as 1 1/2 by 1 1/4 by 1 1/4 inches are commercially available. Use of
such a small transformer will allow it to be hidden behind the false
wall, under a piece of furniture, in the top of a fireplace, or inside a false
ceiling or roof. If batteries are to be used as a power source, be certain
to plan some easy access for replacing them. Installation of feed wires
is best accomplished after the miniature room is completed. Selection
of a wire color which matches the woodwork or decor of the room will
aid in making the wire less visible. Plan the routes for the feed wires
so that they will not be obstructed.

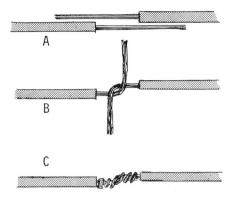

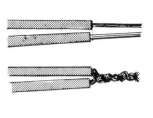

"Pigtail" splice

"Western Union" splice

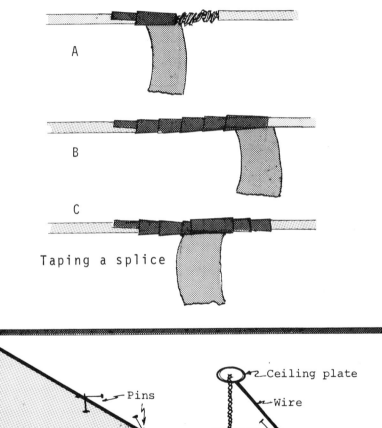

Taping a splice

Ceiling plate

Pins

Wire

Pins

Lamp or
fixture

Installing Ceiling Fixture

You also will have to attach a line cord to the transformer in order to plug it into the wall outlet of your home. This is done by splicing the line cord to the proper wires on the transformer. If your transformer is like that shown in the schematic diagram, it will have only one pair of wires extending from it. The line cord is spliced to these wires. Some transformers have two sets of wires extending from them. One set of these wires should be identified as PRI or primary. The other set should be identified as SEC or secondary. The PRI wires are to be spliced to the line cord. The SEC wires deliver the reduced voltage that feeds the miniature lights. To connect the line cord, use a Western Union splice and proceed as follows:

1) Remove the insulation for a distance of about one inch from the ends of the line cord and transformer primary wires.
2) If the line cord is to go through the side of your miniature room, drill a hole and insert the cord through it before proceeding.
3) Hold one wire from the line cord and one wire from the transformer next to each other, as shown in the sketch "Western Union Splice." Twist the wires across each other, as shown at B and continue wrapping the wires as shown at C. When the first pair of wires have been so wrapped, splice the other line cord and transformer wires together in the same manner. Trim off any excess wire that does not fit into the splice area.
4) Solder the splices you've just made to assure a good mechanical and electrical connection. A loose connection can arc and may cause a fire.

After soldering, each splice must be individually insulated to prevent a short circuit or possible electrical shock to the user. Insulation of the splices is accomplished with vinyl plastic electrical tape. Start wrapping the tape on top of the insulation, as shown at A in the sketch "Taping a Splice." Continue wrapping the wire until the tape extends over the insulation at the other end of the splice. Each wrap of the tape should overlap the preceding wrap by about half the width of the tape, as shown at B. Be sure to stretch the tape and pull it tightly as you wrap. When the first layer of tape has been applied, continue wrapping the tape back in the opposite direction to apply a second layer to the splice, as shown at C. Again, be certain to stretch the tape and pull it tightly as you wrap. Tape the second splice in the same manner.

If your transformer is equipped with mounting feet, it may be fastened in place with screws. Transformers without screw-mounting holes are best fastened in place with silicone cement, the kind used as caulking material.

After the transformer has been fastened in place, proceed with the installation of lights and fixtures. Ceiling lamps should be hung from the ceiling by means of a ceiling plate, a dish-shaped piece about 1/2 inch in diameter which offers a place to hide the splices connecting the lamp wires to the feed wires. Either a jewelry finding or a commercially available miniature ceiling plate may be used. The cavity in the ceiling plate need only be deep enough to hide two small "pigtail"

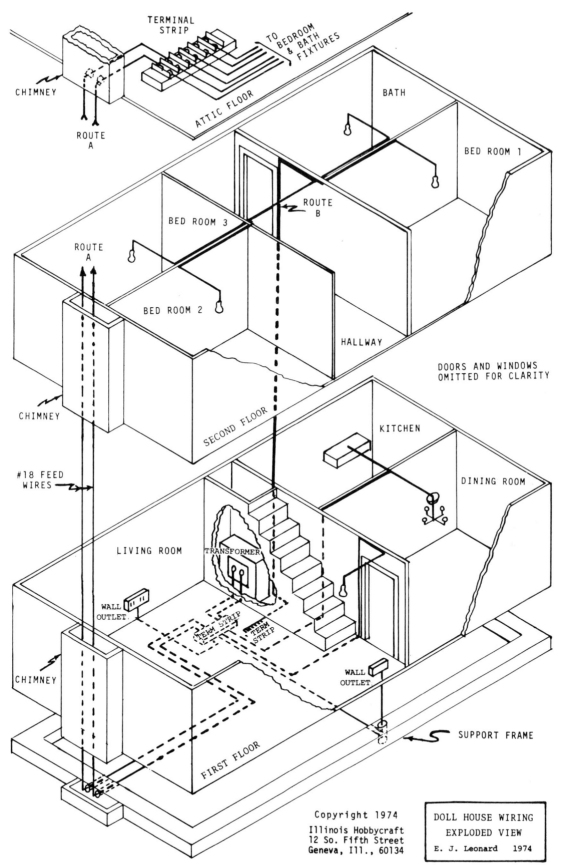

The method diagramed for route "A" can be used if the transformer is located in the attic. In that case, the transformer wires are connected to the terminal strip in the attic, and the feed wires carry electricity to the terminal strip situated below the first floor of the house. Route "B" can be used where the attic is not accessible and the chimney cannot be used to conceal wires. In this case, note that the transformer is located beneath the stairway. *Courtesy: Ed Leonard*

splices. To install a hanging lamp, estimate the length of wire required to reach from the lamp to the power source. Measure and cut two pieces of wire to this length and then splice these wires to the lamp wires by removing 1/4 to 1/2 inch of insulation from the ends of the lamp wires and the feed wires. Slip the ceiling plate over the lamp wires. **Then,** hold one lamp wire and one feed wire side by side, as shown in the sketch "Pigtail Splice," so that the ends of the insulation are even. While holding the wires, twist the bare ends of the wires tightly together. Repeat these operations with the other two wires. Next, solder the wires to assure a good mechanical and electrical connection and cut off excess wire from the splices to make them about 1/8 inch long. Then, insulate the splices. In ordinary electrical work special electrical tape is used to insulate the high voltage (115-volt) splices. However, because these wires are carrying only a low voltage and, in order to keep the splices as small as possible, silicone cement can be used for insulation. To insulate the wires: squeeze a tube of silicone cement so that the cement is forced up into the neck of the tube. Insert one splice into the neck of the tube until the cement covers the entire splice and part of the insulation. Withdraw the wires slowly. Inspect the splice to see that it is completely covered with silicone cement. Repeat with the other splice. Set the insulated splices aside and allow them to dry for at least three hours.

After the silicone insulation has dried thoroughly, slide the ceiling plate out to the end of the wires. Arrange the splices so that they are concealed under the ceiling plate and the feed wires extend out from under the plate in the proper direction. Then, fasten the ceiling plate to the ceiling. Very small nails may be used to hold the ceiling plate in place or it may be fastened with silicone cement. While the cement is drying, the plate may be held in place by "bowing" a thin piece of wood (about 1/16 inch thick) between the ceiling plate and the floor of the room.

After the ceiling plate is securely fastened, the feed wires may be run to the power source via the selected route. If the wires are to go through a wall, a small hole should be drilled through the wall before beginning installation. To run the wire, stretch the wires from the ceiling plate along the ceiling to the rear wall of the room. If the wires are to run along the back wall, insert a straight pin up into the ceiling, close to the wall (as shown in the sketch "Installing Ceiling Fixture") for the wires to bend around. Then insert another straight pin into the wall, next to the ceiling and close to the first pin, to hold the wire tightly against the ceiling. Continue this running and pinning operation until the exit hole or the power source is reached. When the power source is reached, connect the wires to the power source to make sure the lamp operates properly. After testing the lamp, check to see that the wires are taut and held firmly in place all along the run. Apply a coat of Sobo or Elmer's glue or other transparent drying glue over the entire length of the wire where it is exposed inside the room. Allow the glue to dry for at least twenty-four hours before removing the pins.

BASIC WIRING FOR THE BASIC ENVIRONMENT

Basic materials and equipment are assembled—soldering iron, solder, tape, silicone adhesive, bell wire and transformer, bulbs and sockets, switch, tacks, and tools.

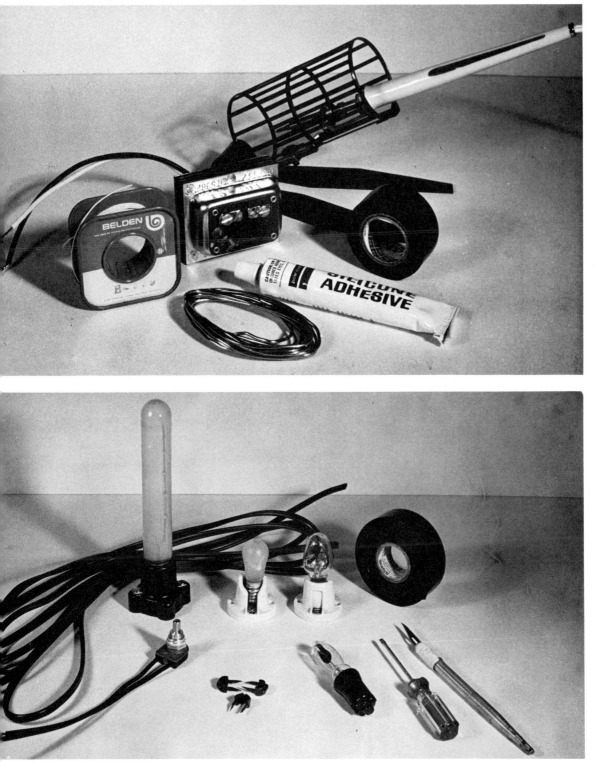

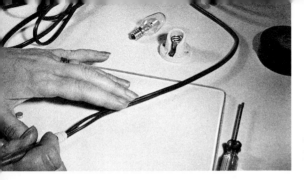

The double wire is cut apart with an X-Acto knife.

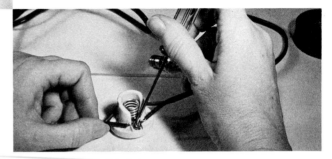

The plastic cover is stripped away from the wire to lay bare a 1-inch section.

The bare wire is separated in half and attached to either side of the fixture and wrapped around each of the screws, and the screws are tightened to hold the wire in place.

The bare wire is taped with electrical tape, for protection.

A complete light attachment.

To attach a fireplace flicker light, unscrew the top part of its socket.

Separate the double wire in the center with an X-Acto knife for about one inch or enough to go around the fixture.

Straddle the screw with the wire and press the wire firmly into the projecting contact points with a screwdriver, making certain that the plastic coating around the wire has been penetrated by the metal points.

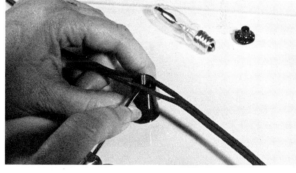

Screw back the back piece to hold the wires in place.

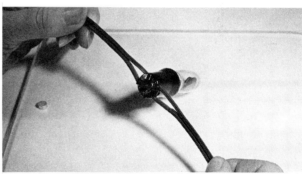

Attach the flicker flame light through the opening left in the fireplace.

This boudoir scene features two Chrysnbon* lamps which have been wired with tiny grain of wheat bulbs. Executed by Betty Leonard, Geneva, Illinois, this room was installed in a box which is only three inches deep and therefore provides no space for concealment of a transformer. *Courtesy: Ed Leonard*

Boudoir scene is powered by a small transformer (foreground) which plugs directly into the wall and therefore requires no space inside the box. Heavy wires leading from the transformer deliver 12 volts and are connected to the lamp wires at the terminal strip which is glued to the back of the box. Wires which feed electricity to the lamps can be seen entering holes just above and to the right and left of the terminal strip. This method of lighting is the simplest possible and requires no soldering or running of wires inside the room. *Courtesy: Ed Leonard*

* Chrysnbon is a registered trademark of Chrysnbon Miniatures, Inc.

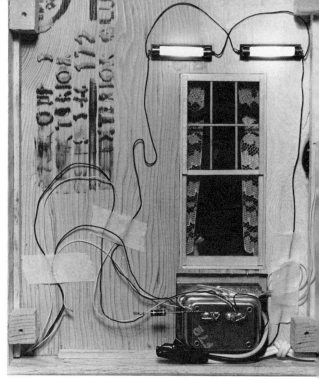

This Christmas scene by Peggy Leonard, Geneva, Illinois, includes four separate lighted elements: the Christmas tree, a village under the tree, a wall lamp and lighting (behind the false wall) for the scene outside the window. The transformer which powers the lights is installed behind the false wall and extends partway into the window seat. *Courtesy: Ed Leonard*

General Store, by Evelyn Franz, Geneva, Illinois, incorporates an accurately scaled "store lamp" from Illinois Hobbycraft. The room's cover frame has been removed to show fluorettes, mounted behind reflectors at front of ceiling, which provide general lighting for the scene. This picture was taken using only the light furnished by the fluorettes and the lamp. This box has no false wall, and the scene outside the window is not lighted. Wiring was done after the miniature was completed. A transformer, located under the counter, was installed through a small door which was cut into the back of the box. Installation of wire in this completed miniature room posed a problem because wires could not be run down the back corners of the room to reach the transformer, as would normally be done. Instead, the groove at the top and left was cut into the edge of the box to accommodate the wires. When in place, the cover frame conceals this groove. Wires from the "store lamp" were fished through a hole in the false ceiling, brought out through a hole at the center top, and spliced to the wires which also feed the fluorettes. Wires leave the groove at the bottom left to run along the left side wall at the floor, and then across the lower back wall to reach the transformer under the counter. *Courtesy: Ed Leonard*

Rear view of Christmas scene shows the wiring and transformer hookup. The heavy cord at lower right corner of the box is the line cord which is spliced to the primary wires of the transformer. The two pairs of wires which enter the hole at the lower left corner supply electricity to the Christmas tree and to the village. The white wires which enter the hole halfway up the right-hand side of the box feed electricity to the wall lamp. Fluorettes, which light the outdoor scene, are mounted above the window and are fed by the black wires running up each side of the window. The tubular device to the left of the terminal screw on the transformer is a resistor which is connected in series with the village bulbs in order to dim them slightly. Wires have been taped to the back of the false wall to keep them from moving around when the box is transported. The back of the box is removable and, when installed, is held in place by four screws which are turned into the four blocks glued in place near the four corners of the box. The removable back facilitates the installation of wiring and provides for access for maintenance after the room is completed. *Courtesy: Ed Leonard*

A collection of miniature rooms housed in a beautiful old
secretary, similar to the 17th- and 18th-century collections
in the Netherlands and Germany. *Collection of Jean Stuart*

3 | KINDS OF SETTINGS

CONTAINERS FOR SETTINGS

Settings, as miniature environments, can be assembled, constructed, or placed in and about a wide variety of containers. The most basic is a box that has been custom-constructed to contain that particular assemblage of materials for the setting. As you have seen in Chapter 2, it can be a very flexible receptacle, accommodating almost any arrangement.

The basic box, however, is not by any means the only possibility. Since the seventeenth and eighteenth centuries in the Netherlands and Germany, cabinets have also been used (along with the dollhouse). Unless there is a covering over the front, keeping the contents clean, an open cabinet shelf can become a problem. When collections were assembled on a cabinet shelf or in a cubicle, pieces were rarely affixed to the cabinet, because there was no good reason to do so. Usually one did not carry around large cabinets to display collections, so permanency of placement was not a consideration.

Some cabinets are so constructed that the interiors can simulate a cross section of a dollhouse interior. Then settings can be designed to

An old wooden kitchen clock case turned into three miniature rooms by Carol Dinkel. *Collection of Ruth Saunders*

A closeup with the clock frame opened up.

Another series of room settings by Carol Dinkel built into a wooden cabinet.

A miniature scene that spills out into the foreground. Japanese Doll Palace. *Courtesy: The Cleveland Museum of Art*

Twentieth-century Japanese model of a No stage with 17 actors depicting a scene from the play *Yuya. Courtesy: The Metropolitan Museum of Art Gift of the Kokusai Bunka Shinkokai, through Setsuichi Aoki, Secretary, 1935*

A fishing shack. *Collection of Elizabeth Ellis*

A diorama showing the founding of the New York Stock
Exchange in 1792. The miniature group is by Ned Burns.
Courtesy: Museum of the City of New York

Radko Dimitrov Degardin depicted by memory the village of his boy-
hood, Bansko, Bulgaria, in miniature (where he still lives). These pal-
ettes, with sections of old Bansko, spilled over into almost every room
of his house. What a beautiful record!

A closer view showing his precise attention to detail
and scale.

Radko Degardin pointing to the room where he was
born.

fill each area in some kind of order or sequence as in a dollhouse, or to depict a series of scenes or historical images of particular periods.

Settings can also spill out onto the surrounding area. This is particularly true of complete buildings such as the Stock Exchange, the miniature Japanese Doll Palace, the Fishing Shack, or Radko Dimtrov Degardin's Bulgarian Village scenes. These approach the idea of a diorama—something one would see in a museum as a display to illustrate a particular subject.

Then, too, there is a unique and imaginative approach—the use of "found" objects as containers for miniature settings. Various clock cabinets such as a cuckoo clock, keyhole clock, and grandfather clock are

Pieces that can hang on a wall. Miniature settings in a keyhole clock. Conversion and interior made by Carol Dinkel.

A clock case of rooms (one could also use the interior of an old radio cabinet), made by Carol Dinkel. Collection of Virginia Merrill.

A cuckoo clock from the 1850s converted into miniature rooms. Made
by Carol Dinkel. *Collection of Jeanne
Knoop*

A cabinet *cum* Victorian parlor.
Collection of Jeanne Knoop

A second-size pine wall cabinet circa 1830, containing an even tinier collection of miniature pieces. *Collection of Jeanne Knoop*

A shadow box conversion into a sitting room and attic. *Collection of Jeanne Knoop*

Cigar boxes used as mouse houses. Made by Jeanne Knoop.

great readymade cases. So are letter boxes, old lanterns, antique glass-doored store display cases, and shadow boxes. Some of these can rest in a cabinet or be displayed on a table or hung on a wall.

More unusual is the fitting of a nutshell, jug, box, barrel, trunk, suitcase, or basket with a miniature scene or a series of scenes.

Old window frames also can become the front cover frames of boxes which then can be fitted with cubicles. Chests with drawers removed, or the fronts of the drawer replaced with glass or acrylic also are great housings for collections or groupings of settings.

Scrounging in a junkshop or in an antiques shop with the thought in mind: "What can I convert into a container for a miniature setting?" will open up a multitude of creative possibilities. Simple adjustments can be made; imagine removing a door, slicing something in half, turning a form upside down, and so on.

SUBJECT MATTER

It is almost foolish to talk about subject matter for miniature settings because the universe is your realm and almost anything we are able

Subject matter can be almost anything. Treatment can be carried out creatively as in "Pour les Dames," a hat shop for ladies executed by Laura Davis for the Beehive Studio, Inc. *Courtesy: The Beehive Studio, Inc.*

People throughout the world make what is most familiar to them. This Batak house from the Lake Toba region of Sumatra, Indonesia, was made by an old man who duplicated the house in which he lives.

A front view of the house which is 12 inches high. The paintings and carvings are all symbolic. At the uppermost peak of the roof is a buffalo head which depicts "fertility and plenty."

Charles Gardner of Stockton, Rugby, England, is a woodworker who collects and refurbishes old gypsy wagons as a hobby. He has several on his property, along with some miniature models. This is one, complete with hand-carved horse. All parts are authentic down to the finest detail.

to see can be miniaturized. There is a good reason, nevertheless, to discourse about content. Most settings fall into the category of room interiors, period rooms. These are staples of the miniaturists' art. A setting executed to perfection is beautiful to see. But how many times do we have to express the same kinds of ideas? Then there are the fads. For example, someone creates a great general store and displays it. After a while, at another exhibition, one sees multitudes of these.

Another of Charles Gardner's miniatures, a gypsy wagon in another style.

The roof comes off to reveal the interior.

A contemporary room, American style, with a conversation pit, stained glass window, and acrylic side chairs and table.

A contemporary room in central Romania. A typical farmer's cottage room complete with storage cabinets and spinning device. The only thing missing is a clay or wood-plank floor. These pieces were made in Romania.

Since the realm of possibility can be infinite, why be repetitive? Why not look to scenes from our contemporary life—images with which we are most familiar—such as a supermarket, a restaurant interior, a beauty parlor, a modern gift shop, candle store, a gift and card store, an office? These are just a few ideas that are presently atypical. The contemporary scene most often appears to be shortchanged (even in this book). Keep in mind that life-styles of today certainly will become the historical records or nostalgic references of tomorrow. Just think of how modern the Victorian-styled interior of a dollhouse appeared to be to the contemporary Victorian. Why does expression of the miniature arts today have to describe in eclectic fashion bits and pieces of yesteryear? For the expression of nostalgia or a certain quaintness? These really are not valid components of an art form—even a folk art form. One must decide whether one's objectives are to display technical prowess with a media, whether the miniature setting is chronicling a past point in time, or whether it will express what we truly know, understand, and have experienced. There is room for both.

A GALLERY OF EXAMPLES

A peddler's cart by Martha Dinkel can stand alone on floor or table and tells its story as an integral unit. *Courtesy: Martha Dinkel of The Mousehole*

Table pieces can be shallow vignettes as in this letter box with paper figures made by Elizabeth Ellis.

This egg is a real one, cut open and decorated to reveal the fantasy of a skating scene. It is a table piece in the collection of Elizabeth Ellis.

This table piece opens from the back and is in the collection of Mrs. John McCown.

Another table setting in the collection of Mrs. John McCown.

A carousel that plays carousel music as it turns, by Brilar. It sits on a table as part of Elizabeth Ellis's collection.

A corrugated box can become a miniature starter.

A crude box with ceramic figures. Scenes from the folk
artists' environment in the mountains of Peru.

A permanently sealed lamp base by Mary Jones. *Courtesy: Mary Jones*

Another lamp-base scene in miniature depicting *Alice Through the Looking Glass,* inserted by Mary Jones. *Courtesy: Mary Jones*

One of a series of shallow vignettes (8 inches X 10 inches) that can hang on a wall. "Potting Shed" by Muriel Hoffman. *Courtesy: The Beehive Studio, Inc.*

An 11 inch × 14 inch three-dimensional "picture" " 'Twas the Night Before Christmas . . ." by Laura Davis. *Courtesy: The Beehive Studio, Inc.*

A look into a country store. *Courtesy: Green Door Studio*

This piece can sit on a table or shelf. An antique shop in the
collection of Gloria Hurme.

The inside of the antique shop with the front opening like
a door.

The exterior window of Dayton's Dry Goods Store in Minneapolis, Minnesota in the year 1907, made by Eugene Kupjack.

And another aspect of the Dayton's Dry Goods Store by Eugene Kupjack, an interior view.

A greenhouse from Mary Jane Graham's *It's a Small World.*
Courtesy: Mary Jane Graham

A Chippendale setting from *It's a Small World. Courtesy: Mary Jane Graham*

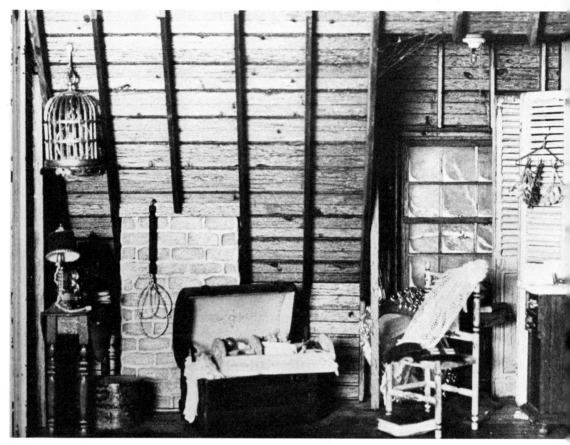

An attic from *It's a Small World. Courtesy: Mary Jane Graham*

A bathroom made by Elizabeth Scull.

A miniature antique shop in the collection of Alice Knauff.

A closeup of the antique shop. This is a good way to put together a collection of sundry miniature pieces that otherwise don't belong together.

A French pastry shop in the collection of Elizabeth Ellis.

A general store containing over 500 items. This is another
way of "containing" a collection. Made by Jeanne Knoop.

A look into a flower shop from *It's a Small World. Courtesy: Mary Jane Graham*

A miniature English Pub by Antoinette Barloga of Craft Patterns. The piece is wired so that the fire in the fireplace glows, the Christmas tree lights up, as well as the lantern and sconce. *Courtesy: Craft Patterns, A Neely Hall Production*

While in a cast from shoulders to ankle, recuperating from an automobile accident, high school student Stephen Le Clair made the parts for this general store. He shaped the meats, crocks, and so on and his mother fired them in a kiln. She brought them back to his bed, and he painted them. Mr. Atkins of The Village Smithy sold Stephen's pieces and also made the weathervane that is on the roof.

Another way to put accumulated collections into perspective—an antique shop. *Collection of Elizabeth Ellis*

"Ark of Noah," by the Rochester Folk Art Guild, combines a high level of craftsmanshp with art and history to create this miniature. Is it a sculpture, a three-dimensional illustration of a biblical story, or is it a toy? *Courtesy: Rochester Folk Art Guild*

Another creation by the Rochester Folk Art Guild, this time a tree is hollowed out and fitted to make an imaginative "Astrologer's Tree House." *Courtesy: Rochester Folk Art Guild*

A quarter-size Queen Anne lowboy in mahogany made by Paul A. Runyon to duplicate exactly a full-scale piece in every detail, all the way down to the basic construction of joints and so on.

This William and Mary highboy, second size, in walnut, made by S. A. Raube, is exactly like a full-size piece in construction details, except for a simulated burled effect that was achieved through use of paints.

This globe looks like the real thing, however, only in outward appearance. The globe does not turn. Made by Virginia Merrill

4 | HOW TO MAKE MINIATURE FURNITURE

THREE APPROACHES TO MAKING MINIATURE FURNITURE

Creating furniture for miniature settings can take three main routes. The ultimate achievement is to create furniture exactly as an original is constructed. The other two possibilities are to improvise. By taking shortcuts on construction techniques one ultimately can end up with a facsimile that looks almost precisely like the full-sized original (if you don't examine construction details minutely). Or, when using found objects, one can convert them, recombining parts or applying "cosmetic" treatment through surface alterations and thereby producing another type of effective result.

Most miniature furniture is constructed directly of wood, but metals such as wire, and plastics of various types (particularly acrylic and foam) have potential as well. If one is a beginner in working with furniture, it is advisable to improvise and employ simple construction techniques such as butt joints instead of mortise and tenon, and so on. As proficiency increases, more complex processes can be adopted. Of course, upholstered furniture can even have a base of heavy cardboard, but usually balsa or basswood is used because they easily are carvable and pins can be used to hold fabrics in place.

This walnut pump organ with mirror looks like an organ, but none of the parts can be operated. *Courtesy: House of Miniatures*

A complete improvisation by Virginia Merrill. The chess pieces, serving as bases, are ivory, purchased as part of an incomplete chess set at an antique show. And the tabletops are lapidary ground gemstones.

SELECTION OF WOOD

Let us start from the ultimate accomplishment and then look at other possibilities. A cabinetmaker would ordinarily use solid wood where there are curves and where there is the need for carving, and veneers on other parts that have straight surfaces. Since scale is a primary consideration, wood grain texture is significant. Fine-grained woods look best. Lemonwood, lime, pear, beech, sycamore, Cuban mahogany, American holly, spruce, walnut, ebony, cocobolo, elm, and osage orange are woods that work well as veneers and in solid form. Woods such as teak and some coarser-grained mahoganies are not so effective. Decorative face veneers usually are available in 1/28-inch thickness.

On the next level, one can use basswood as a solid. It is a hard wood with a nondescript grain and will cut in any direction. Basswood works well and can be finished to resemble other kinds of wood. Plywood and balsa can also be used for furniture that will end up with an opaque finish. (Walls, roofs, and other flat members of a setting are usually made of plywood. Plywood is available in thicknesses of 1/32 inch, 1/16 inch, 3/32 inch, 1/8 inch and up.)

HAND TOOLS FOR THE MINIATURE MAKER

s = standard work
a = advanced work

Measuring Tools

- s   metal ruler
- s   divider and compass
- a   micrometer—used to measure minute distances
- a   vernier caliper—used for inside and outside measurements and transferring the dimensions to another object
- s   combination square—used for 90° and 45° angles
- s   magnifier on a stand and for head over eyes
- a   contour marker—tiny needles adjust to contours and shape can be transferred to other pieces

Clamping Tools

- s   bench vises
- s   hand vise
- s   improvised clamps such as paper clips, binder clips, hair clips, rubber bands, clothespins, etc.
- a   Pana Vise—vacuum based
- s   spring clamps
- s   C-clamps—various sizes
- s   tweezers
- s   pliers—round nose, chain nose, flat nose

a   forceps
a   a "third hand"—clamps on a base

Cutting Tools

s   wire nippers
s   knives—all types, many from X-Acto and Stanley
s   single-edged razor blades
a   mat knives
a   paper cutters
a   circle cutter (X-Acto)
s   metal snips—combination
s   scissors—cuticle, decoupage, embroidery, and other larger sizes
s   small saws—coping saws and fretsaws, piercing or jeweler's saw, hacksaw, keyhole saw
a   miter box saw
a   razor saw—40 teeth to the inch, very fine
s   ripsaws and crosscut saws
a   chisels—in various blades (X-Acto)
a   gouges—chisels with concave blades
s   carving tools—small-sized chisels and gouges often used for wood block and linoleum block cutting
s   scrapers—flat and beveled-edged in various contours for scraping surfaces of wood and plastic smooth
s   files—jeweler's file assortment and larger assorted shapes
a   planes—assorted small-sized planes for smoothing surfaces (Stanley)

Other Tools and Materials

s   hammers—10-ounce hammer
s   screwdrivers—standard and Phillips
s   jeweler's screwdrivers—small assorted blades
s   spatulas—oil painting sizes
s   assorted dental tools—old ones, perhaps from your dentist
s   sandpapers—garnet, wet-or-dry, aluminum/oxide, silicon carbide
s   drill bits—assorted sizes
a   polishing buffs
a   centering punches—for starting holes for drills, nails, or screws; also for burying nailheads in wood
s   adhesives—Weldwood, epoxies (various kinds from putties to clear), white glue (Elmer's, Sobo), white glue for textiles (Velverette), rubber cement
a   wire benders—bending jigs or dies

Miscellaneous Materials

s/a   solders—hard and soft
s   brushes—various sizes

s acrylic paints
s varnishes—e.g., shellac
s mixing cups and bowls
s wax paper and polyethylene sheeting
s masking and cellophane tape
s toothpicks, applicator sticks, tongue depressors, and coffee stirrers
s jars
s paper toweling and rags
a foam rubber scraps (keep clamps from marking) or flannel-
   backed adhesive
a asbestos sheet for table
s screws and nails—smallest possible
a architect's pencil and sharpener

POWER TOOLS FOR THE MINIATURE MAKER

Tools and Machines

s portable hand drill
s drill press (Dremel)
s jigsaw (Dremel)
a band saw
a portable saber saw
a circular saw (bench mounted)
a radial arm saw
a portable orbital sander
a belt sander (portable or bench mounted)
a jeweler's lathe
a router-shaper
a jointer-planer (bevel mounted)
a grinder
a strip heater (for bending acrylic)

Accessories

s drill points
s cutters
s grinding wheels
s polishing buffs
a rotary files and burrs
a soldering iron

Multipurpose Machines for Light Work

Dremel Moto-Shop—jigsaw, sander, grinder, buffer, flexible shaft
drill and accessories, can be connected to a variable speed regula-
tor

Unimat (American Edelstaal)—lathe, table saw, grinder, drill press, and portable drill

Hand-held 1/4" portable drills can be fitted with various accessories or even can be bench mounted—can be a drill, router-shaper, drill press, grinder, cut-off saw, saber saw, orbital sander, buffing wheel

KINDS OF TOOLS

Jewelers' tools such as jewelers' saws or fretsaws are excellent for cutting wood parts. Dremel has a whole series of tools that provide a complete workshop for the miniature maker. The Dremel Moto-Shop, complete with saw, sanding and polishing attachments, and flexible shaft tool, is excellent. All kinds of burrs and accessories, such as sanding disks, saw, and buffing wheels, can be used in the flexible shaft tool to carve, cut, create joints, sand, buff, etc. (Dremel makes these too.) Speed can be regulated with a variable speed foot pedal leaving both hands free to work. Dremel also puts out a drill press that is just the right size for drilling holes. Their router and new lathe are also useful.

A jeweler's lathe is also a fine machine for turning wood members such as furniture legs and chairbacks. And, of course, various shapes of knives, razor blades, linoleum cutting tools, tweezers, small clamps, hair clips, dental drills and tools, rubber bands, large paper clips, applicator sticks or toothpicks, tongue depressors, or decoupage scissors —are all important to have nearby for various operations. And jar lids are fine to have handy for mixing up small batches of glue or colorants. There are tools made specifically for work on miniature forms. Tools sold to dentists, jewelers, clockmakers, surgeons, and electronics firms are of top quality and wonderfully adaptable. A look into catalogs keyed to these fields will reveal a multitude of tool "temptations."

An architect's pencil that can be kept sharpened to a very fine point with its companion sharpener.

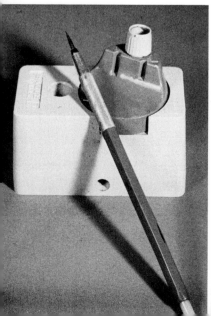

Assorted rulers with fine calibrations and a small T-square.

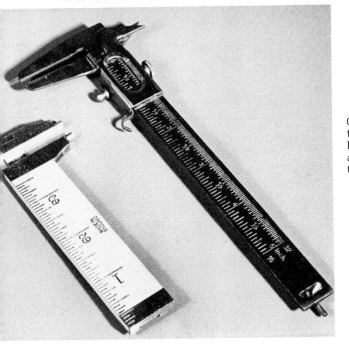

Calipers to measure external and internal dimensions so that these can be transferred to another piece, such as being certain all legs of a table are the same width and length.

Fine wire nippers and dividers. The dividers can also be used compass-style to score a piece of wood or paper.

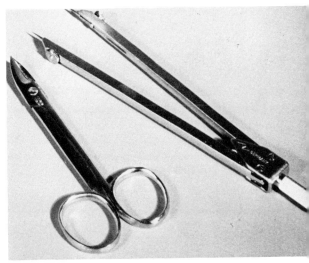

Various kinds of jeweler's pliers.

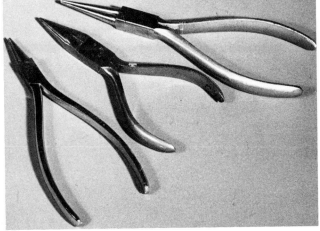

Various types of clamps.

Two versions of Panavises that can be mounted to a spot temporarily, via suction.

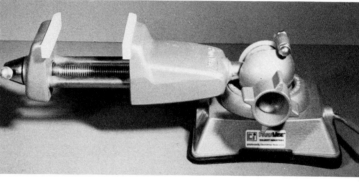

A set of "miniature" turning tools (Brookstone #U-1337.5).

Assorted dental instruments.

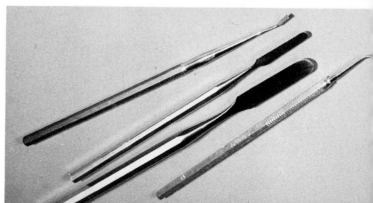

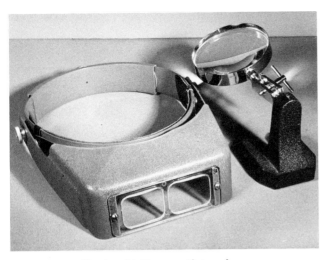

Head and table magnifying glasses.

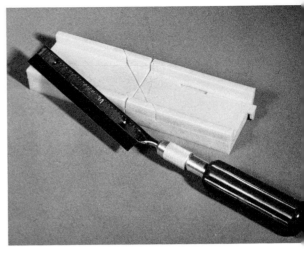

Miniature miter box and saw (by X-Acto).

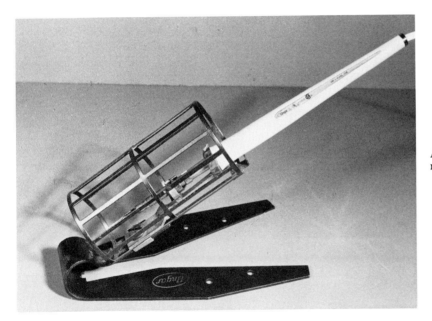

An Ungar soldering iron for miniature work.

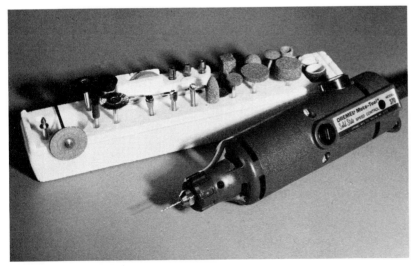

A variable speed Dremel Moto-tool (Model 370) with attachments, used for various drill, carving, grinding, and finishing operations.

125

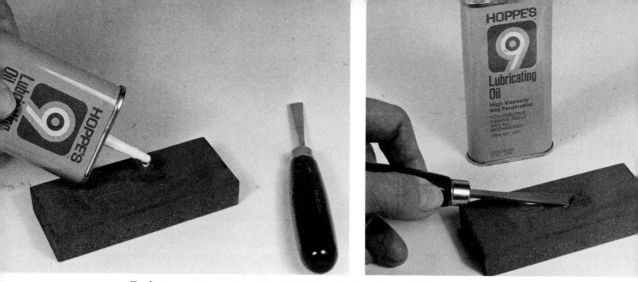

To sharpen cutting and carving tools, deposit a few drops of lubricating oil on a sharpening stone and with the flat of the tool resting on the stone move the tool in a circular motion until the blade is sharpened.

GENERAL WOODWORKING OPERATIONS

What tools to select for cutting wood depends upon the thickness and hardness of the wood. Veneer is usually cut with a veneer saw which looks like a serrated knife blade, with X-Acto knives, knives set into a mat cutter, razor blades, or on the Dremel Moto-Shop saw which has a very fine blade, or the Unimat.

Other woods of varying thicknesses can be cut with a jeweler's saw, fretsaw, band saw, or on the saw of the Dremel Moto-Shop. Complex curves and very small parts require the use of jigs, clamps, and vises in order to hold the member in place—particularly if duplicates need to be cut, such as table legs.

A basic piece of basswood for a wardrobe is cut with a jigsaw, as on the Dremel Moto-Shop, or small table saw as on the Unimat table. Then, an edge is carved with a file.

Door pieces are also cut from a pattern but, since the door units are complex, the internal panel designs are traced from a template and cut out with a saw.

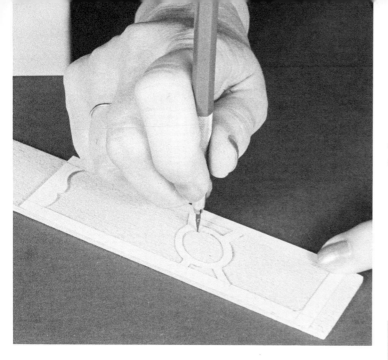

The outside molding is also traced from a pattern . . .

. . . and cut on either a Dremel Moto-Shop saw . . .

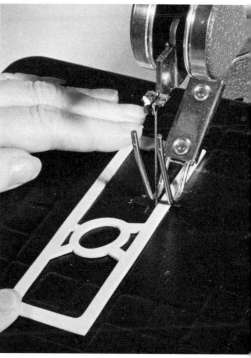

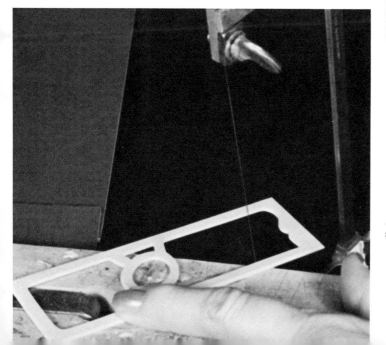

. . . or by hand with a jeweler's saw (as seen here) or with a coping saw.

All units are glued to the background piece using a two-part clear epoxy. (White glue such as Sobo or Elmer's, or Weldwood can be used as well.)

Six layers of veneer are laminated with two-part epoxy and then edges are carved to shape with a knife or wood carving tools.

After all main parts are assembled, with decorative findings glued on the panels, the cabinet is stained and finished with five to six coats of varnish and finely sanded between coats. Then hardware is attached and we have the completed French Provincial style wardrobe.

USE OF JIGS

Jigs are vital devices created for the specific task of holding small parts or members in place for cutting, drilling, routing, and finishing operations. Without these aids, parts would slip out of place, or would be difficult to standardize. In themselves, jigs can be as much a work of art and invention as the finished piece. It is not unusual for a maker of miniature furniture, such as Paul Runyon, to create a dozen jigs for a single piece of furniture.

The most common kind of jig is a holder made by slotting, lengthwise, a piece of wood and placing a stop ¼ inch from the end on each side (to hold it in the vise). When the member is placed in the slot and the jig is placed in the vise, the pressure of the vise clamps the tiny part firmly in place for various operations.

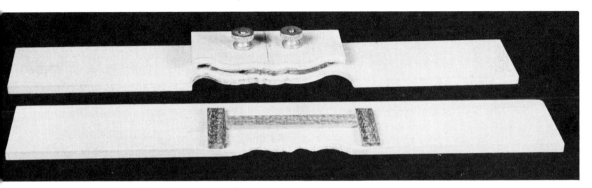

Some pieces of furniture require dozens of jigs. But once a set of jigs is made, the piece of furniture can be reproduced over and over again.   This is a jig made for routing out a complex curve on a router.

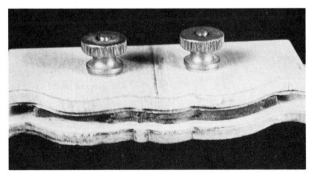

A closeup showing the top and bottom parts of the jig and the sandwich of wood that has been routed. Note that on the left a piece was cracked off. This sometimes happens when there is a fault in the wood.

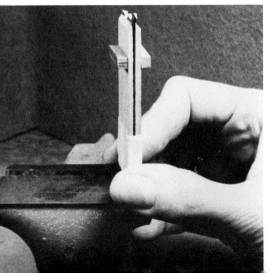

This is another type of jig, shown in profile, a kind used to hold tiny pieces firmly so that various woodworking operations (such as filing and cutting) can be performed.

The jig in its vise, with the tiny wood element ready for woodworking operations.

A closeup showing the stop on the jig to keep it from sliding downward in the vise.

A spool is being drilled with a Dremel Moto-Tool in order to accommodate a plant later. Drills are also used to make holes for jointing such as dowel holes, dovetailing, and tongue-and-groove work. Another use is for attaching hardware and fixtures.

DRILLING

When drilling holes into small pieces of wood with hand or power drill, the wood should be clamped into place and the drill bit should be held straight (at a 90° angle to the wood). After the spur of the bit breaks through the wood, pull out the bit and turn the work to the other side to complete the hole. This will prevent the wood from splitting or splintering.

130

FASTENING AND ATTACHING MEMBERS

Fastening or attaching members of a piece of furniture is accomplished mainly with adhesives and the use of dowels and special woodworking joints. Nails or screws are very rarely employed. The most common adhesive is a white glue, polyvinyl acetate, or chloride, which is sold under many trade names such as Sobo, Elmer's, etc. Powdered glues such as Weldwood, urea-formaldehyde resin glue, and casein glues, are more waterproof and stronger and are used for adhering larger pieces. Epoxy resin adhesives, sold in two-component packages, are also excellent for attaching dissimilar materials such as glass or metal to wood.

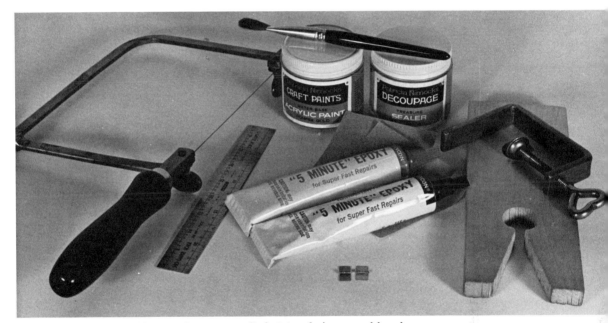

Tools for assembling a cabinet are readied. A jeweler's saw and bench pin *(on right)*, glue, sandpaper, hinges, and finishing materials.

All parts are cut from basswood using patterns. The two parts shown here are door units. They are attached temporarily onto the front doors with a dot of white glue. They act as a temporary gauge so the doors can be fitted properly into the cabinet. (They are removed afterwards.)

All parts are attached with white glue. This is the cabinet top which is 1/8th inch thick. Other parts are of 1/16th-inch basswood.

Hinges are attached after sealing the wood and painting the cabinet with acrylic paint. (The 17th-century Chinoiserie designs are painted on the parts before hinges and handles are added.)

JOINTING

An integral aspect of fastening parts together is the art of jointing. Whether you use butt joints, mortise and tenon, dovetail, dowel pin joints, dado joints, or the many variations of these, depends upon your skill. Drills, routers, and flexible shaft tools equipped with various bits are used to create joints. The diagrams shown here describe some more applicable joints, progressing from the simple to the complex.

132

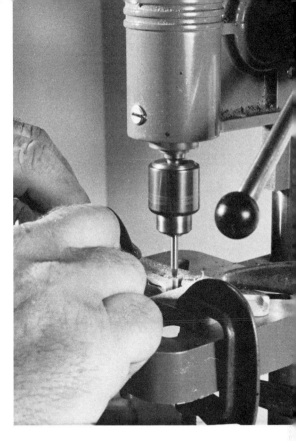

(Above and right) One type of tongue-and-groove joint. Grooving is done with a drill press using dental burrs.

Another type of tongue-and-groove joint. This is common for attaching table frames.

A dovetail joint used often to attach drawers, sides of cabinets, boxes and so on. Dovetailing is done in a drill press using dental burrs.

A leaf support attachment for a gateleg table, showing mortise (slot) and tenon. The tenon is shaped on a router.

133

MOST COMMONLY USED JOINTS IN MINIATURE FURNITURE MAKING

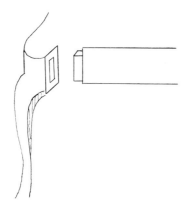

MORTISE AND TENON

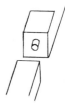

DOWELED JOINT

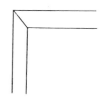

MITRE CORNER

LEG IS TAPER SLOT-DOVETAILED TO CENTER PILLAR

LAP DOVETAIL OR HALF BLIND DOVETAIL

A blanket chest in cherry wood showing dovetail joining.
Chest is by Donald C. Buttfield.

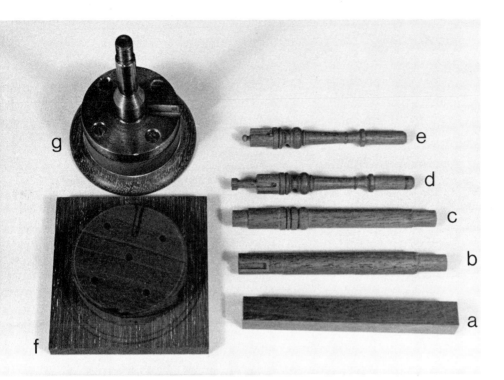

Wood sizes vary from 1/28th inch thick to 9/64ths of an inch. Here Paul A. Runyon shows the first stages in making his tilt-top table. Stages (a to e) are steps in shaping the shaft from a rectangular piece of Cuban mahogany to the slotting of the joint on a drill press using a dental burr, to the shaping of the table's shaft (on a jeweler's lathe). The square piece with drilled circle (f) shows the original square piece of wood (with turning outline in pencil) prepared to receive the face plate for turning. And (g) illustrates the turned tabletop with face plate attached.

After the tabletop is turned, it requires reinforcing. The two long pieces of wood, called "cleats," are screwed to the underside of the top, across the grain, to prevent warping. (The tiny screws are called crown screws and are usually flat-bottom screws used for eyeglass frames. Mr. Runyon grinds ends into points.) These cabriole legs are hand carved. They are dovetailed into the base of the turned shaft using the device shown next.

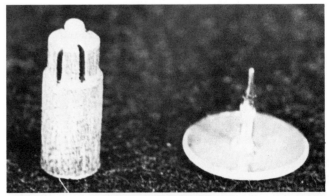

This is a dowel with slots to receive the cabriole legs. The tack shows comparative size.

Paul A. Runyon's Queen Anne style tilt-top table. The fine-grain Cuban mahogany is finished with five coats of shellac and dry-sanded with #400 Tri-M-ite Fre-Cut finishing paper (an open coat). Then #0000 steel wool is used for the final finishing followed by a rubbing with paste wax or French polish.

A view of the table back tilted upward.

Measurements: width 1 1/2 inch for the tabletop; height 2 1/16 inch. It is very difficult to discern, without some other object present to define its scale, that this remarkable, precisely made table, is so very small.

MAKING A CABRIOLE LEG

Another master miniature maker is Donald C. Buttfield. Here is a sequence of steps showing the making of a cabriole leg. After starting with a rectangular piece of wood, a slot is made by drilling little holes in a row, one next to the other. The shape of the leg is drawn on the wood using a template. The fourth and fifth steps *(from the left)* show what is cut away with a hand coping saw. The final two shapes are carved with hand tools and then sanded.

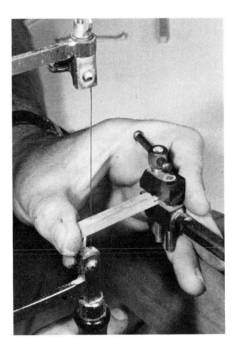

Mr. Buttfield cutting away excess from the cabriole leg-to-be. Note the kind of vise he uses.

The cabriole leg used in this Queen Anne style handkerchief table of cherry wood. By Donald C. Buttfield

Another use for the cabriole leg in this chess table with an inlaid top of holly and rosewood. By Donald C. Buttfield

VENEERING

Veneers usually are glued to a base such as plywood or, more practically, basswood. White glue (or Weldwood), clamps (cramps) are necessary here. Try to keep glue off surfaces that are to be finished later with stains or varnishes because glue spots can cause uneven color absorption resulting in surface discoloration. If you should find some glue on the wrong surface, wash it away with a sponge, water, and a bit of vinegar. You can also stain surfaces before gluing. Any jointing should be done before veneering.

Pattern veneering is created by matching veneers for making designs or patterns. If two or more leaves are taken from the veneer bundle in strict order, they can be matched as in a book, quartered and matched, diamond quartered by cutting four consecutive leaves diagonally, or side matched and butt matched, or even matched in herringbone fashion. Traditional furniture surfaces employed frequent use of pattern matching.

After gluing the veneer and base surfaces, the veneer is tamped in place with a roller or brayer moving it in zigzag pressure applied to distribute and remove excess glue. Butting edges are masked together with masking tape. Clamps (which are essentially strips of wood that sandwich the veneered piece between them and are held firmly at each end with C-clamps) are used to hold the veneer securely in place while the glue is drying.

A basswood base, veneers, veneer saw, white glue, and sandpaper are on hand for the veneering of a potential tabletop.

The design is drawn as guidelines with pencil on 1/8-inch basswood—that side eventually will become the bottom.

Using the table saw of a Unimat, the saw is set to accommodate the 1/28th inch thickness of the veneer, and the piece is run through following the guidelines. (A hand drill with templates acting as gauges can work as well, particularly for curved shapes.)

A check of the grooved lines. The width of the cut from the saw blade will determine the width of the inlay.

Using a veneer saw, the strips for inlaying are cut with the grain. These pieces and background are stained before putting them into place. (If glued before staining, excess glue would inhibit staining by acting as a resist.)

White glue is run along the groove lines of the basswood and the strips are placed in the grooves. A rubber mallet is used to tampen the pieces farther in place. The glued piece is allowed to dry overnight.

Excess off of the edges is trimmed with a saw. The piece is varnished with five coats of Dura-Fame (or comparable varnish) and dry-sanded, using #220–400 grit wet-or-dry sandpaper, and then refined further with #0000 steel wool. The result is a table or cabinet top.

An antique second-size desk with a wood inlay design around the drawers and desk flap. *Collection of Susan Richardson*

CARVING

Carving is accomplished by gouging and cutting away solid wood surfaces with linoleum cutting tools (which look like miniaturized sculpture tools). Burrs of various configurations are also good carving tools when used in a flexible shaft tool or in a Dremel Moto-Tool. The more one cuts into the wood the greater the resulting relief. Scale must be considered when carving into a wood surface. Sculptural elements must be in proportion to the whole.

BENDING

Veneers can usually be shaped with the grain by just gluing and clamping them to curved surfaces. But if thicker woods are to be curved or bent into extreme curves, they should be steamed or soaked in hot water and then clamped to a mold using tension straps, masking tape, or metal around the top part over the moistened wood and forced by clamping into the mold (or caul). The dampened wood, when dry, will assume the new shape.

Curved laminated wood members can be formed by gluing together several pieces of thin veneer with the grain running in the same direction. These are then clamped in a rigid form until the glue dries. Laminated curved wood is stronger than solid curved wood.

Although all wood can be bent or sprung to some extent, where extreme bends are necessary in solid stock, only hardwoods such as oak, elm, ash, basswood, hickory, or beech should be used. High-density wood is desirable. Defects such as knots or surface checks can cause failures. The wood will just crack and splinter.

Green stock, unseasoned, bends more easily and requires heating only to prepare it for bending. Seasoned wood, on the other hand, requires some moisture and heat. When the wood is both wet and hot its plasticity is increased.

The usual practice is to steam the wood in a box into which you can feed wet steam (as from a teakettle) or to submerge the wood in hot, boiling water. The amount of time the wood should be soaked depends on the hardness, greenness, and thickness of the wood. A general rule of thumb is about one hour per inch of thickness.

After the wood has been softened, the stock should be bent as quickly as possible to minimize the loss of heat and moisture from the inner and outer surfaces.

Mild bends can be made over frames or forms without using a strap. One end is fastened in place and is then pulled against the mold form and clamped at intervals. Or, if the piece is very small, it is necessary to clamp only the ends.

If the bend is severe, then a strap with end fittings or blocks to restrain the tension side (outside part of the bend) should be used. The tension straps must be fastened at both ends of the bent section with clamps or some other device.

To fix the bend permanently, the wood must be cooled and dried under tension. It should not be removed from the form until dry.

Materials are assembled for making a chair of wood with a formed (bent) back. On the right are the basswood pieces.

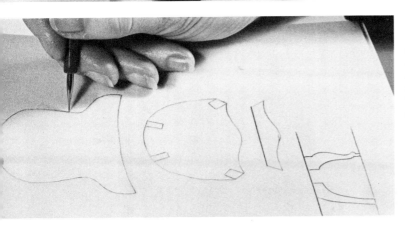

The parts of the chair are drawn on tracing paper.

Using a stylus, the design is traced over carbon paper onto the wood. Another approach is to make a template out of bristol board and use that to draw the contours of each piece.

Another way is to use a Dremel Moto-Shop saw, as seen in the cutting of this chair back. Note that the grain of the wood runs up and down from the top of the chair back down to the bottom (and not across), to facilitate bending later.

The seat is cut with a scroll saw.

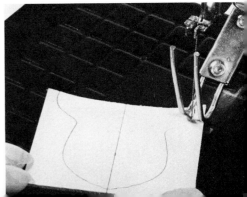

The legs are traced in 1/4 inch thickness of basswood so that curves can be carved and sanded to create the final curved shape.

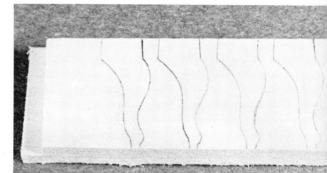

The chair legs waiting to be carved into rounded shapes.

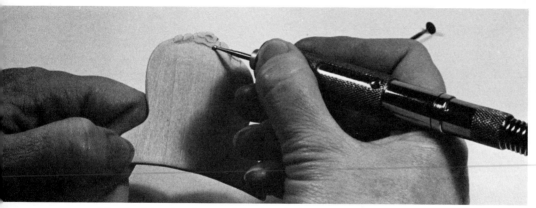

The floral detail at the top of the chair back is carved with a dental burr in a flexible shaft tool . . .

. . . or with a rounded bit in a Dremel hand drill.

With the carving completed, the chair back is soaked in very hot water until it is bendable. The amount of time for soaking depends upon the thickness of the wood.

The now flexible wood is bent around a jar that has the proper diameter ...

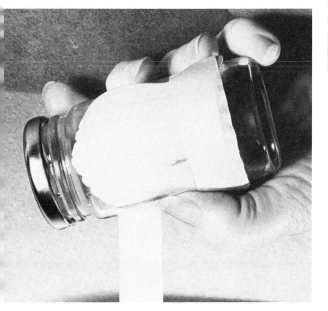

... and it is taped in place and allowed to dry overnight.

Pieces are assembled and glued with white glue or Weldwood and then stained. The chair seat could later be upholstered with a cushion.

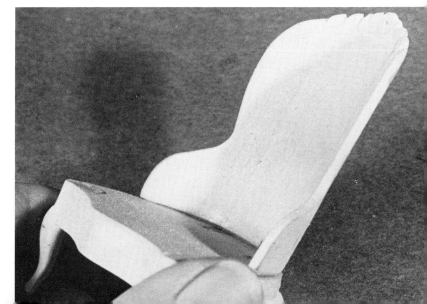

TURNING

Turning of miniature forms can be accomplished between centers on a jeweler's lathe (or the new Dremel miniature wood lathe) using linoleum carving and metal carving tools. To turn a chair leg, the length of wood is centered and mounted to both ends of the lathe. A triangular pointed tool is then used lightly to remove square corners, roughing

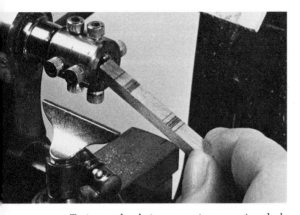

To turn a leg between centers on a jeweler's lathe, the rectangular piece of wood is pinned between the centers.

With miniature turning tools, the square edges are cut away first, until the piece is dowellike in shape. Then designs are cut into the piece. A rest is used to help hold the tool steady. Note the original turned model above. Calipers are used to determine and compare distances so all the legs finally turn out to be the same shape.

The drill end of the lathe is fed into the blunt end of the turned chair leg to form the slender dowel shown in the next illustration.

The turned form now has a blunt end that is ready to be shaped.

down and gradually cutting away wood until the form is round, while the lathe turns at medium speed, or start with a dowel which is already round. Then, by applying various parting tools to areas, the leg can be tapered, or shapes, such as beads, can be cut into the surface to vary the pattern.

Because parts are so small, a lathe can be improvised by clamping a hand drill to a rigid surface using a screw mechanism to hold the wood in place in the drill and by allowing some freely rotating pin to be mounted into a support at the opposite end. Rotation should be toward you.

Turning an empty thread spool on a jeweler's lathe to make a table base or a vase.

This is a new low-cost lathe (#700) put out by Dremel and designed especially for the miniaturist. *Courtesy: Dremel Manufacturing Co.*

Besides being able to "turn" between two centers on a lathe, it is also possible to do "face plate" turning. Here a square of basswood, temporarily attached to a face plate, is being placed on one center for face plate turning (to form a tabletop).

After the square corners have been cut away, leaving a round shape, the curved outer molding is turned. Note how the tool is held and poised on the rest.

A "bird cage" type of tilt-top table in black walnut made by Donald C. Buttfield.

INLAY: INTARSIA AND MARQUETRY

Inlaying is the overall term denoting the practice of inletting one material of a different color, texture, or composition into another. *Intarsia* is the introduction of mother-of-pearl, brass, silver, bone, ivory, or wood into a ground. Outlines are traced on the ground with a fine point, and recesses to accommodate the piece to be introduced are cut into the wood with wood carving tools. The new part is then glued into the recess. Mother-of-pearl can be inlaid by heating it in boiling water for ten minutes and then when soft cutting it to shape with a scissors.

Marquetry is a later development of inlaying which employs freer use of form using various colored veneers which are cut out from a

Mother-of-pearl inlay in a miniature musical instrument from the collection of Elizabeth Scull.

Two other miniature instruments also inlayed with mother-of-pearl from the House of Miniatures. *Courtesy: House of Miniatures*

A marquetry design inlayed into a dining table.

pattern and then closely juxtaposed jigsaw-puzzle fashion so that no space is apparent between shapes. The pieces are then glued to a base. Veneer is usually 1/28 inch (1.5mm) or less in thickness. After adhering it to the base, the thickness can be reduced by sanding in a circular motion.

OVERLAY WORK

Wood or metal laid over but not inserted into a ground is known as *overlay*. Examples of these are frets on Chippendale cabinets and metal embellishments on Directoire pieces. When applying embellishments, to keep the glue from oozing out and marring the surface so that the adhesive does not permit the stain to absorb, roll out glue on a flat surface, press the attachment onto the glue, and quickly transfer it to the ground. Pin it in place, if possible, or weigh it down with a heavy object.

FINISHING

Refining the furniture surface to a final texture and color is the finishing process. It may involve scraping, sanding, buffing, and applying various colors and sealers, such as stains, opaque color, wax, linseed oil, shellac, lacquer, or the new plastic-type finishes such as acrylic, vinyl, or polyurethanes.

SCRAPING

In a jig and/or vise, individual parts are scraped with a metal wood scraper until smooth. When joints are completed, they are also leveled with a scraper.

SANDING

Sanding is performed during various stages of the finishing process —after scraping, after applying a filler, and after using hard surface finishes.

Usually 320 grit to 400 grit Tri-Mite sandpaper is used dry, along with 0000 steel wool, to bring the wood furniture surface to a fine high gloss finish.

OTHER FINISHING OPERATIONS

Wood surfaces require sealing. If the wood is to be stained, a weak stain is brushed or rubbed on. Most stains act as sealers. When that has penetrated and dried, a 30% shellac to 70% alcohol wash coat of shellac is painted on the surface. This seals the pores enough to keep the filler from darkening.

Then a paste filler, colored to match the furniture color, is applied to fill in any rough areas as well as the joints. When the stain has dried, three to five coats of shellac are applied very, very fast with no overlapping with a good clean brush. (It is best to apply shellac in a nonhumid atmosphere.) The shellac should be not heavier than half-and-half cream and no thinner than milk. A good grade of alcohol is used to dilute the shellac. After each coating has dried, the surface is sanded with 400 grit Tri-Mite, Fre-cut open coat finishing paper, and finally with #0000 steel wool. A waxing with paste wax completes the job.

It is also possible to apply oil finishes. Watco and Vitroseal are two kinds of oil finishes that can be brushed on. There are also very good waxy stains such as Miniwax. These oil and/or waxy stain finishes act as sealers as well as finishes.

Other hard finishes are applied in very much the same way as the shellac, but when different finishes are employed, use a compatible sealer first.

Whatever finish one uses, the surface must be refined and very smooth because of the need to consider every aspect to scale.

Materials are gathered for making a three-panel room divider or screen. A Persian miniature print is cut to match the size of the basswood panels. Hinges and finishing material are also on hand.

All surfaces of the basswood are sealed with a wood sealer. When dry, the panels are sanded dry with #200 grit wet-or-dry sandpaper.

Elmer's Glue-All is diluted with a bit of water and brushed evenly onto the surface of the wood.

Starting at one end, with corners fitting squarely, the print is placed on a glued surface. Air pockets are carefully smoothed out with fingers and then lightly rolled with a brayer. Do not press too hard, or else you will remove too much glue.

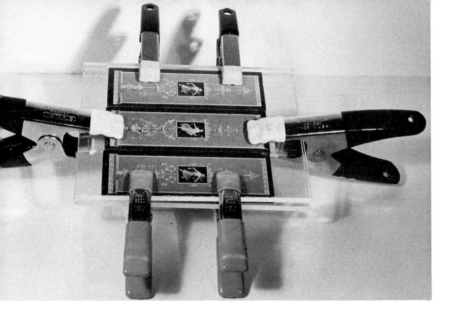

Although not the screen shown in this series, this technique should be helpful. After the paper is rolled on, allow the piece to dry while clamped between a sandwich of acrylic. This prevents warping. Warping tends to occur because stress is placed on one side of the thin wood.

The back of the panel is covered with lining paper and, when that has dried, both the front and back are painted with eight applications of polyurethane varnish, (McCloskey's Dura-Fame) with fine wet sanding (#400) between every two coats. The final finishing is completed with a rubbing of #0000 steel wool and a coating of paste wax.

The completed three-panel Persian print screen.

A miniature decoupaged wardrobe. The painted coating is acrylic paint. And except for painted border designs, the animal and floral forms are cut from paper and glued to the acrylic surface with white glue. Many coats of varnish are added, sometimes enough to actually bury the paper in varnish. Then sanding to a satin-smooth, unblemished surface completes the operations.

Another miniature wardrobe in the decoupage style.

ATTACHING FINDINGS

Miniscule findings require miniscule drill bits in order to make holes to attach screws or pins for holding hinges, drawer pulls, knobs, and

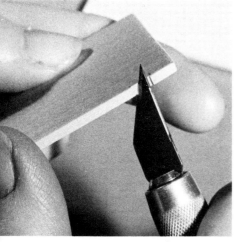

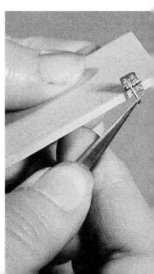

In order to attach hinges to doors, screens, boxes, and similar hinged parts, a tiny sliver has to be cut out of the wood in order to accommodate or recess the hinge. This is done quite easily with an X-Acto knife.

Using a pin vise (miniature hand drill) that rotates when pressure is applied, holes are made in the wood to attach the hinge.

Brass sequin pins that match the tiny brass hinges are inserted into holes with a two-part epoxy. The pins are then permanently glued in place.

the like. A bit of glue on a pin will secure it. Another alternative is to glue the finding in place—but not on a waxy or oily surface. If a piece is to be waxed or oiled, affix the finding before staining or waxing.

Here is a lovely screen with too-big hinges. They are out of scale.

Paul A. Runyon hand cuts (with various jeweler's cutting tools) his own metal findings such as this drawer lock.

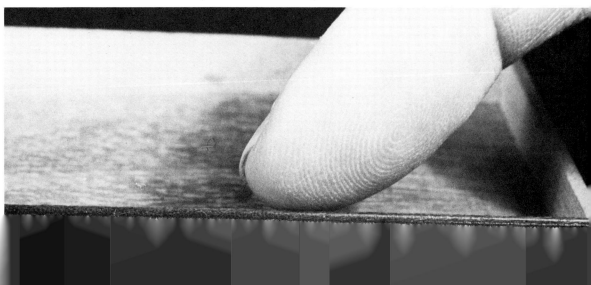

IMPROVISING

With imagination, many objects created for other uses, or as cast-away pieces, can become useful appointments for the miniature environment. For example, a wooden thread spool can become a flowerpot, candleholder, footrest, bench, table base, umbrella stand, and so on, depending upon what is cut or sanded away, how much is drilled away, or whether a cushion is applied to the top.

Costume jewelry pieces very often can function as accessories or parts for accessories. Chess pieces can become pedestal bases; coasters or poker chips can be used as tabletops. Similarly, lamps and chandeliers can be made from jewelry elements. Charms, particularly with movable parts, can become the silverware, sculpture, or table decoration of a room. Use of pill capsules, thimbles, buttons, scarves—are just some of the improvisations that are revealed throughout this book. A creative look without preconceived ideas of a part's function will help you make useful discoveries.

PAUL A. RUNYON—A MASTER'S APPROACH TO MINIATURE FURNITURE MAKING

Many of the photographs shown here reveal a cabinetmaker's approach to furniture construction. Mr. Runyon creates a piece of furniture using exactly the same procedure as for constructing a full-sized piece. The result is a true-to-life working replica in miniature.

One of Paul A. Runyon's early pieces; a dry sink made from pine. *Collection of Ruth Runyon*

He always begins by drawing plans to scale, followed by constructing the individual parts along with attendant jigs. Solid woods and
veneers are used just as in the original. Members are scraped and
sanded. He even makes scrapers to fit certain shapes. Jointing also
mimics the full-sized version. Tongue and groove, mortise and tenon
joints are made with drill bits and dental burrs. White glue is sometimes used. Other times Weldwood is applied in a 70°F room and left
to dry under pressure overnight. Weldwood doesn't show the joint
lines when joints are well fitted. After parts are assembled, findings are
often turned on a jeweler's lathe. Finishing is also an elaborate process,
much like the steps described under "Finishing."

A Paul A. Runyon clock that actually runs. The cabinet is
solid mahogany with a boxwood inlay. Hardware is solid
brass, turned and otherwise made by Mr. Runyon. The
clock face is hand-painted paper over metal.

A carved shell design in the style of Queen Anne chairs, of
Brazilian walnut. Chairs by Paul A. Runyon. Petit point
seats by Virginia Merrill.

Captain's chairs and table of pearwood by Paul A. Runyon.
All parts are constructed as a full-sized set would be made.

The top part of this comb-back Windsor chair was steam
bent. The Sheraton chess table and chair are of satinwood.
Made by Paul A. Runyon. *Collection of Ruth Runyon*

A mahogany dining table by Paul A. Runyon extended
with a leaf added. Brass tips for the legs were hand-formed.

An underside view showing the extension mechanism of
Mr. Runyon's dining table. It is difficult to believe that it
is 1/12th inch scale.

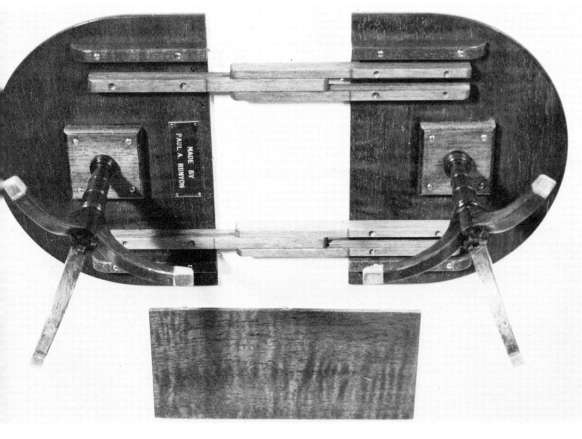

A Chippendale blanket chest in mahogany by Paul A. Runyon.

A spice cabinet by Donald C. Buttfield in 1/12 inch scale (as are his other pieces).

A Queen Anne lowboy and corner chair by Harry Smith.
Courtesy: Harry Smith

Two chairs and a lowboy by Betty Valentine.

A Queen Anne tea table by Fred Shubert.

Basin stand and corner chair by Eric Pearson. *Collection of Jean Zenker*

160

Chair and table by Edward G. Norton.

Chair and desk by Edward G. Norton.

Antique slat bed (craftsman unknown). *Collection of Eleanor
McCown*

Collection of furnishings from *It's a
Small World. Courtesy: Mary Jane
Graham*

Box 1 1/2 inches long. Made by
Virginia Merrill.

Mahogany table by Virginia Merrill.

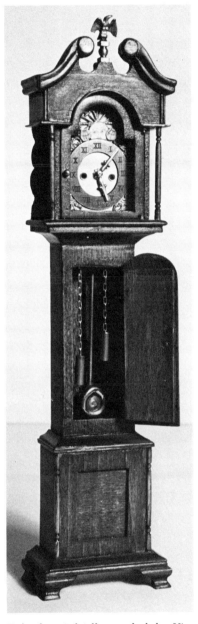

Federal period tall case clock by Virginia Merrill. *Collection of Susan Richardson*

A kitchen sink in walnut put together with dowels.

163

WORKING WITH ACRYLIC

Acrylic is an amazingly versatile material. It is a thermoplastic that can be softened and shaped with heat over and over again. It comes in sheet, fusible pellets, and liquid form for use as coatings, adhesives, modeling pastes, gessos, and paints.

It is quite simple to cut, drill, and adhere acrylic. The usual woodworking and metalworking processes and tools would suffice. Acrylic can be cut with a jeweler's saw, band saw, saber saw—in fact, any saw. It also can be cut by successively scoring a deep line into the sheet and snapping it apart.

Although there are special drill bits that drill beautiful clean holes into acrylic, regular metalworking or woodworking drill bits would suffice.

Acrylic can also be shaped with heat by applying a heat source until the acrylic reaches the softening point and then folding or bending the sheet to the proper configuration using a jig. When acrylic is soft enough, a metal or wooden mold form can be pressed into it (or the reverse) and when the acrylic cools (which is in seconds) a new shape will be given to this marvelous material. A homemade strip heater* can be made to heat bend lines, or heat from the top of a broiler unit will also work. Acrylic can be adhered to itself by applying ethylene

*A Rohm & Haas product that can be bought from most shops that sell acrylic. See "Supply Sources."

AN ACRYLIC MAGAZINE RACK

Making an acrylic magazine rack requires five small pieces of acrylic 1/16 inch thick cut to size, masking tape, and a syringe for delivery of the acrylic cement (methylene dichloride).

A steel wood scraper is used to scrape away saw marks from edges while the piece is securely mounted in a vice.

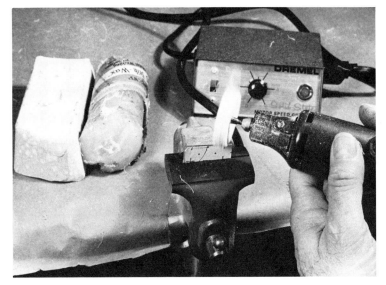

ges that will be exposed (not glued) are pol-ned with a cotton buff wheel that is dressed ith tallow and buffing compound. The Dre-el rheostat unit lowers rpm's so the wheel es not build up heat and friction to melt and m up the polishing operation.

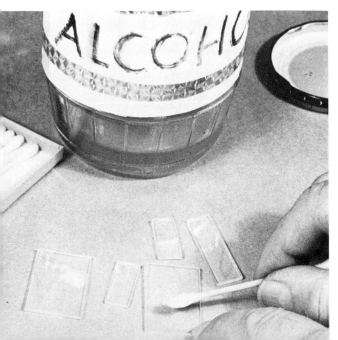

The masking paper is removed and any grease or markings are cleaned away with cotton swabs and alcohol.

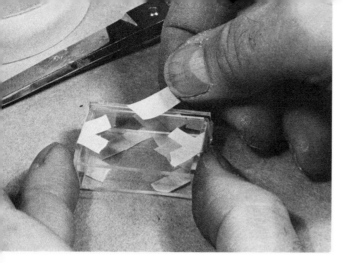

After cleaning, parts are placed in order for gluing by taping Xs across joints.

With a polyethylene syringe charged with methylene dichloride, a bead of the clear liquid flows down the seam, softening the plastic and then, when dry, fusing the joints.

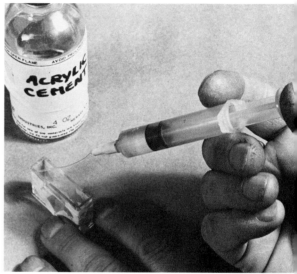

The completed magazine rack, one inch tall, by Thelma R. Newman. Magazines come from Shackman's.

dichloride to the surfaces to be adhered using a syringe or brush as a dispenser. This solvent cement softens the edges and in seconds, as the solvent evaporates, the acrylic forms a strong bond.

Finishing acrylic to a high polish is also possible by scraping edges with a metal scraper while the acrylic is held in a vise; by sanding the acrylic successively with 240- to 400-grit wet-or-dry sandpaper using it wet to help dispel buildup of heat; and by buffing the part with buffing compound (used for metal) and a loose muslin buff in a wheel running at slow speed. Scratches and other kinds of surface marring can be buffed away. Johnson's Pledge or paste waxes will maintain the acrylic surface.

Acrylic is even clearer than glass and can be used as a substitute for glass. Other uses for acrylic in the miniature world are for boxes, bowls, lamp parts, furniture, doors and windows (bay windows can be curved using acrylic), and so on.

A CONTEMPORARY ACRYLIC CHAIR

Forming a contemporary acrylic chair requires the making of a model and an appropriate pattern.

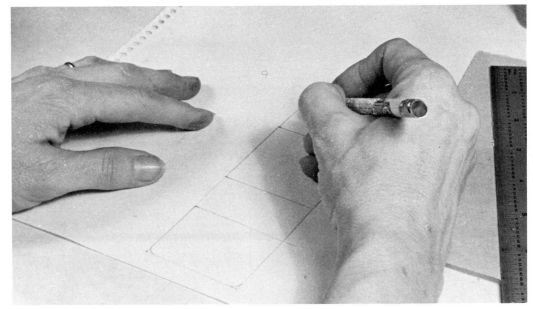

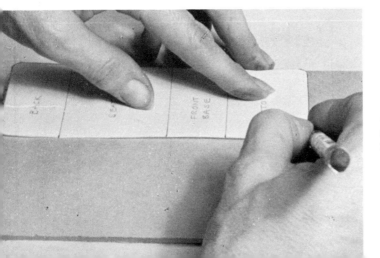

The pattern is labeled and its contours are traced directly on the protective paper of the 1/8-inch acrylic sheet.

Contours are cut on a Dremel Moto-Shop saw.

Saw marks and roughness along the edges are scraped away with a steel wood scraper while the acrylic is mounted securely in a vise.

Next, edges are sanded wet with #400 wet-or-dry silicon carbide (sand) paper.

168

The edges are brought to a high shine by buffing on a wheel. When using this type of wheel, do not allow the tops of edges to touch the wheel, else the piece will fly out of your hand.

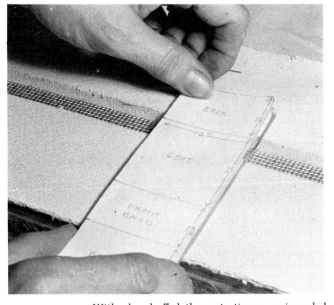

With edges buffed, the protective paper is peeled away from the acrylic and the piece is placed on a heating strip for softening. The pattern is there temporarily just to gauge where the fold line will be. Wherever the acrylic is heated, it will soften and bend.

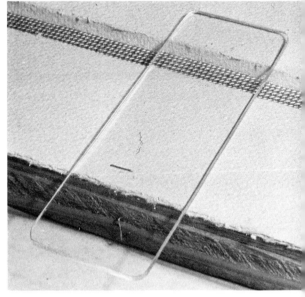

When softening has occurred, a change in the surface will become visible almost as a ripple.

169

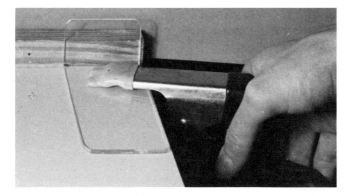

When sufficiently soft, the acrylic is removed from the heat strip and quickly folded and clamped in a jig.

A second heating, softening, and bending operation occurs and then a third until ...

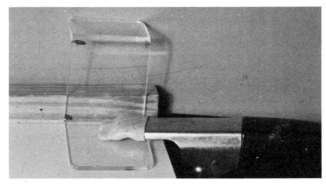

... the chair has been completely formed. It is 1 1/4 inches from floor to seat. By Thelma R. Newman

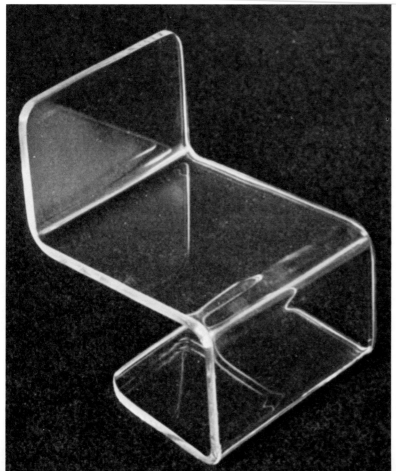

Some acrylic miniature furniture in clear and smoke plastic by April Day Creations. *Courtesy: April Day Creations*

Another acrylic grouping. *Courtesy: April Day Creations*

WORKING WITH PLASTIC FOAMS

Plastic foams are expanded from various plastics. The most commonly known are the polystyrenes—a familiar trade name is Styrofoam®—and polyurethane foams. Foams can be either rigid or soft and have a wide variety of applications as wall and partition materials, furniture and pillow materials, and as the carvable base for bathroom and kitchen units, to name a few possibilities for the miniaturist.

A foam core material, which is a sandwich of foam between two pieces of a Bristol-board-like material, can be cut, pinned into, and painted, thus becoming an excellent structural material, particularly for walls, staircases, and ceilings.

Expanded rigid polystyrene foam (Styrofoam) and other similar foams can be cut with a heated nichrome wire and modeled with a heating pen or small soldering iron, as well as with knives and razor blades. Parts can be adhered with Sobo, Elmer's glue, or similar cements. Rigid expanded polyurethane also can be cut and adhered the same way.

Soft expanded polyurethane is best cut with a Dremel Moto-Shop saw or a band saw. Knives and scissors work also but are more difficult to use for exacting work because the softness of the foam offers no resistance to the cutting blade. These foams can be adhered with white glue or rubber cement.

Rigid foams can be coated with acrylic modeling paste, sanded smooth when dry with wet-or-dry sandpaper, and brush-coated to a fine finish with layers of acrylic gesso. Acrylic paint can become a finish coat as a colorant. A hard, smooth surface is possible using these materials. Because foams are porous, parts can be inserted easily with a bit of hand pressure or use of a fine drill bit.

Flexible foam is great for upholstery because of the ease of fitting fabric to the foam with pins, adjusting fabric shapes with scissors, and then, by slicing into the foam, adding a bit of glue along the cut, the fabric edges can be tucked away without a stitch.

An assortment of various kinds of foams. Some are rigid, others solid, some are finely textured, others coarsely textured. The two most useful are those of the polystyrene family (Styrofoam) and those great polyurethane foams.

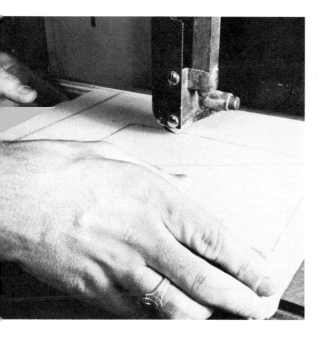

Foams can be cut with a knife or with any kind of saw, particularly on a band saw as shown here . . .

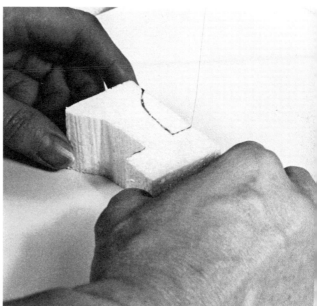

. . . or with a hot wire cutter. The basic cubelike piece was cut from expanded polystyrene packing material (found in a typewriter package). The contours of a bathroom sink were drawn on the foam using a marking pen, and then the foam was cut with the hot wire (heated nichrome wire) cutter.

Refinements and details were completed with a heating pen (used to draw on wood). Note the asbestos pad under the piece.

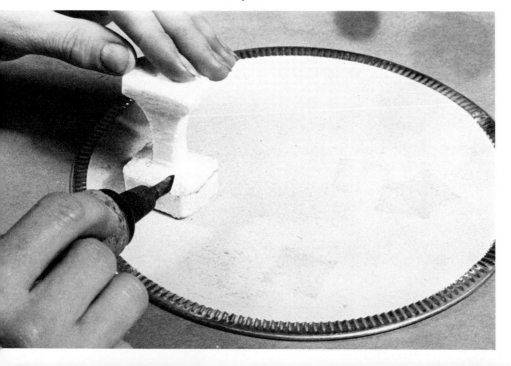

Acrylic modeling paste was modeled over the rough foam
with a palette knife to fill irregularities in the surface and
to create a smoother texture.

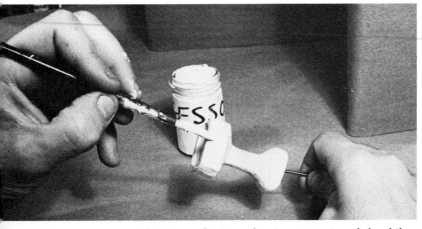

After two applications, the piece was wet-sanded and then
coated with two coats of acrylic gesso. The gesso, when dry,
was sanded until the surface became smooth and glasslike.

After the gesso dried (in about five hours) holes were
drilled into the sink to accommodate the fixtures.

The cast lead fixtures (brought from miniature accessories houses) were inserted with a touch of white glue. The drain, by the way, is a rivet.

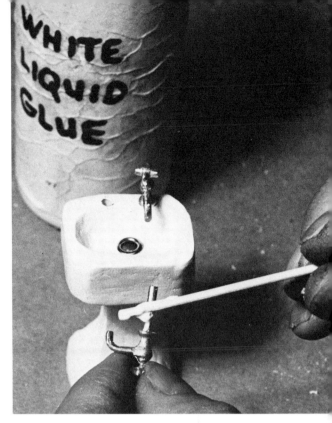

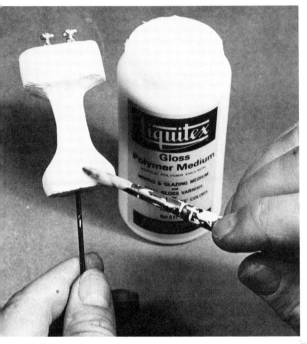

Finally the surface was treated to a final gloss coating of acrylic medium. It acts as a glaze or varnish.

The completed sink.

Fine lace can be used for accessories. Elizabeth Scull made
these from old lace. The silver is by Eugene Kupjack.

A finely croucheted afghan from the collection of Elizabeth
Scull.

5 FABRIC AND PAPER APPLICATIONS

OVERVIEW

Fabrics used to make rugs, draperies, upholstery, wall coverings, quilts, can be basically the same in texture and pattern as those used for the full-scale version except, of course, in relation to scale. If ready-made textiles are used, one must look for very tiny patterns and very fine textures. There are new synthetics and some low plush knits that function beautifully as floor coverings and upholstery materials.

Virtually all the needlework and hand textile-making arts are applicable if one scales down needle, thread, background, and pattern, whether the textile design is structural, integrated into the weave, or nonstructural, superimposed on the textile surface. It is possible to create miniature batiks by applying wax with the tip of a toothpick on a fine fabric to resist dye. Tie-and-dye can be made by sewing and wrapping areas of fabric using needle and thread before dyeing the fabric. Weaving can be accomplished on a makeshift loom constructed from a box. The warp must be close and fine, and the fine yarn or thread used as a weft tightly battened together with a fine reed or baby comb.

Embroidery, including all canvas embroidery such as petit point and

A miniature working loom, 8 inches high, from Mexico, that is capable of producing fine plain weaves.

Finely woven fabrics and lace were impregnated with wax in order to maintain the sense of action that the fabric imparts to this form from southern Mexico.

More finely woven textiles, to scale in texture, and impregnated with wax.

Linen-drawn work towels. Made by Elizabeth Scull.

Hand weaves in Colonial overshot patterns are made by Lillian A. Gaines. *Courtesy: Lillian A. Gaines*

bargello, as well as drawnwork, appliqué, patchwork, quilting, and the like, are made virtually the same way but would easily tire a good pair of eyes. Knitting and crocheting are also possible, using ultrafine tools.

Petit point has great potential, as demonstrated here, and is popular in the miniature world because it has many applications, as carpet, upholstery, pillows, and as wall or screen decorations.

There is a correlation between design and the process or technique used to create textiles. The act of applying a resist to a textile, whether it be a paste or wax resist, helps govern the design quality of that fabric. Weaving of a tapestry causes unique treatment of shapes and their juxtaposition, inasmuch as distinct areas of color have to be connected in some way to neighboring shapes, else large slits would result between areas and the textile could lose its shape after hanging awhile. Petit point requires employment of single stitches, each a tiny unit that makes up a whole; therefore, each spot of color is at first an integral spot, very different, for instance, from a printed calico where colors can blend.

Even though textile design is influenced intrinsically by its materials and processes, so are relationships of material and process extrinsically different.

HISTORICAL INFLUENCES

Designs of different periods and places can vary greatly, or be greatly influenced by borrowings from one culture to another. Some designs maintain an isolated uniqueness, as exemplified by the reverse appliqué molas of the Cuna Indians, or the tapa cloth designs of the South Pacific. Other designs weave throughout centuries of textile history. The weaves and prints of the Orient—China, Persia, and India—were traded in the Near East shortly after the time of Christ. They were collected by the Crusaders, later copied by the Renaissance craftsmen, and are still surviving today, two thousand years later. The rosette, artichoke motif, and palmette are typical of these designs. Lozenge shapes appeared on the quilted robe of an Egyptian Pharaoh and later on the quilted vests of Crusaders. The seed pod, symbol of fertility of Kashmir, India, became an integral part of the beloved paisley of the seventeenth and eighteenth centuries in Europe and America.

In time, design became less geometric and more naturalistic as processes were refined and new yarns, dyes, and machines were introduced. Brocades, for instance, were made possible by the invention of the Jacquard loom.

FABRIC CHOICES

As in any of these newer techniques, particularly the knitted and nonwoven synthetic fabrics of today, there are always qualifying elements. This is what has to be considered in choosing a fabric wisely or custom creating textiles for a specific use. For instance, small details that might look well on smooth surfaces cannot translate successfully to roughly textured surfaces. In silk screening or block printing a fabric, the size of the screen or the block should enter into considerations of design.

And certain designs were more popular during certain periods and were reflected in the environment as curtains and draperies, wall, furniture, and floor coverings.

An assortment of fabric swatches showing some designs
and textures applicable for miniature applications.

The great challenge for the miniaturist is searching for appropriate
textiles for all kinds of environment applications. Where proper designs, textures, and scale cannot be found, the only other alternative is
to make your own weaves, petit point pieces, or prints.

There is much improvising necessary in finding knitting needles
small enough in scale—they could be made of rigid wire; or locating
a weave fine enough to silk screen a fabric, and so on. Adventure into
the wide range of possibility offered by the textile arts requires further
investigation into each area—and then the inventing of adaptations.
Only some are indicated here.

ADAPTATIONS

Making of Rugs

Because scale is so critical here, invention is a requirement. How
does one create an Oriental rug to scale with authentic color, texture,

MAKING A RUG FROM A SCARF

Making a rug from a woman's challis scarf in a paisley design requires a minimum of materials and no stitching. The scarf, iron-on adhesives, strips of linen, Elmer's Glue-All, and an iron are all that are needed.

The scarf is cut to the proper size and pattern. In this case the border and a center design are utilized.

Parts, overlapped slightly, are glued together with a white glue.

A border is added that will be folded under part of the way.

The glued-together sections are tacked with pins to a board in order to stretch and shape it. One-side iron-on fusible web is cut to what the actual size of the rug will be. It acts as a backing and helps the rug to lie flat.

The backing is pressed in place.

Two-sided fusible web is placed on the border. And then the border is folded over and pressed.

Fringing, which is actually a strip of natural plain weave linen, is glued in place with Elmer's Glue-All or Velverette.

From scarf to carpet.

Another carpet made from a scarf.

and design? Rugs could be woven as they were for Queen Mary's Dolls' House, or rugs can be created through canvas-based embroidery such as petit point, or converting textiles such as scarfs into rugs. Of course, the most satisfactory, and impossibly long approach is to weave the rug, but these other improvisations work out very well. A step-by-step approach for using both of these methods is described here with photos and their captions.

It is also possible to braid rugs, particularly when designing a Colonial American interior. The process is simple and exactly the same as making a full-scaled piece except for the thickness of the yarn or, if a rag rug, the thickness of the fabric strips.

Hooking rugs are also the same in process as the normal-sized version, except that a very, very fine crochet hook is used and, of course, the pattern is reduced proportionately.

Wall-to-wall carpeting and broadloom area-type rugs are easy to make. There are elegant shallow-plush knits, velvets, and the like that are available for tacking or gluing to the floor.

A RUG FROM A RIBBON

Rugs can also be made from finely woven ribbons. For this type, cut five pieces—one for the center and four outside trapezoid shaped pieces with mitered (45°) corner angles.

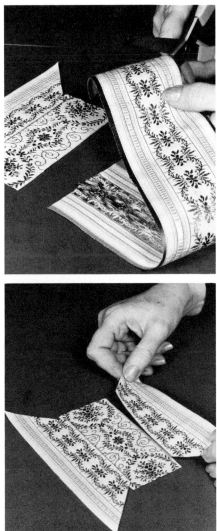

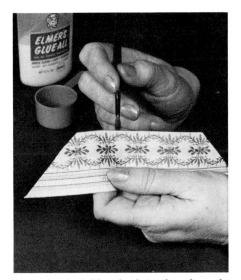

Run a bead of diluted white glue along the raw edges to keep the fabric from fraying.

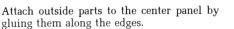

Attach outside parts to the center panel by gluing them along the edges.

The completed carpet made from ribbon.

MAKING A PETIT POINT RUG

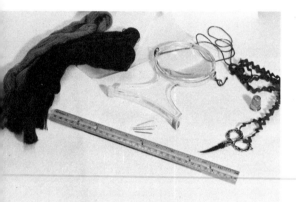

Materials and supplies are gathered for making a petit point rug.

A basic continental stitch.

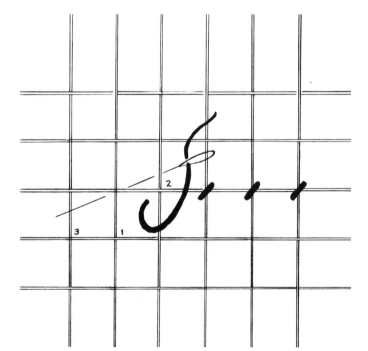

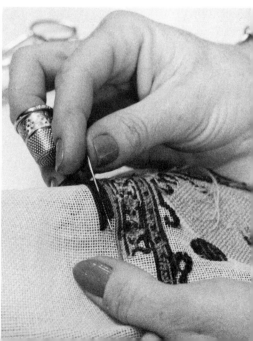

A cotton 24 mesh is excellent for miniature petit point rugs, and a very fine Persian yarn is used. Here Jean Jessop is ending a thread.

Blocking a petit point rug by pinning it to a board so that
corners are squared. Dip the rug in warm water first. If it
is soiled, use some Woolite in the water.

A petit point rug by Jean Jessop.

Elizabeth Scull's petit point rug made in DMC cotton in a Greek key design.

A petit point "Oriental rug" by Chestnut Hill Studio.

These petit point rugs are made by Kate Marks.

A petit point rug by Susan Richardson.

A petit point rug by Deborah McKnight.

Carpeting an area requires cutting the shallow plush fabric to size, adding Velverette (fabric) adhesive to the floor . . .

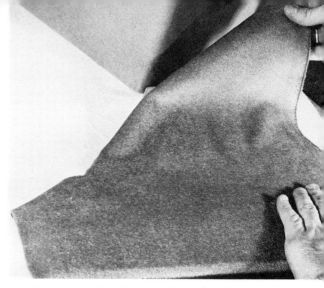

. . . and stretching the fabric tautly while pressing out airbubbles. The shallow stairway on the upper left was simple to do because this low-pile fabric had a knit, slightly stretchable backing.

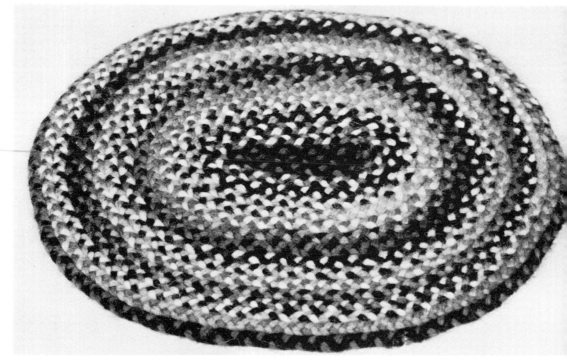

A wool braided rug 5 inches X 3 inches by Carol Dinkel.

Curtains and Draperies

Curtains and draperies are more easily adapted than the rug because a broader range of texture and pattern is available. Silks, in their various weaves, cottons as solids and prints, fine wool such as challis, as well as a host of fine sheer weaves and fine laces are possibilities. Of course, one is likely to find these textiles in the fine quality dress fabric department of fabric shops rather than where heavier and coarser

190

fabrics are sold. Don't forget to look at what is being sold in the handkerchief department. Handkerchiefs often are very finely made and can be converted easily into curtains.

The making of draperies can circumvent the usual processes through the use of the new iron-on webbings. As you can see in the illustration

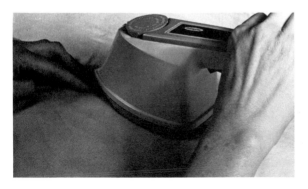

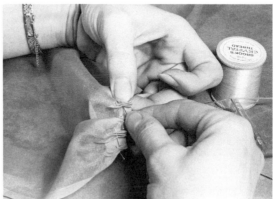

To make wall-to-wall curtains (or draperies), a strip of fusible web is ironed onto a fine silk organza along all four edges with the edges folded under.

Triple tucks are taken at the top for the drapery folds and temporarily pinned.

The tucks are tacked with clear nylon sewing thread.

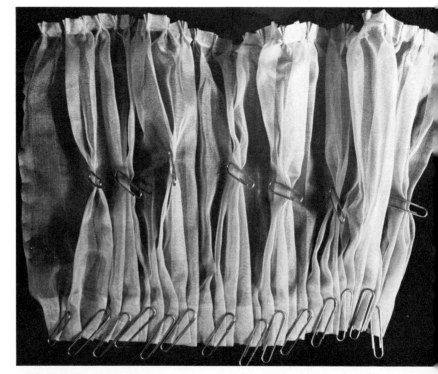

Then the tucks are pulled tautly and fastened with paper clips. Eventually, two by two, the tucks will be lightly steam ironed. The completed curtains are in the modern room in Chapter 3.

here, it is possible to whip up draperies without using a stitch. Scissors, the iron-on webbing and white glue for fabric (Velverette), fabric, trim (optional), and background are all that is needed. If fabrics are the right texture and pattern but the color is off, why not dye the material the color you need?

After curtains and draperies are made, a valance is usually cut and covered to hide the top pleating. Then this entire unit is glued to the window or window wall.

Curtains are also made by threading a "rod" with wire or string tautly through a channel left in the top of the curtain.

Draperies and curtains for large window expanses can be made by sewing pleats in the top of the fabric as an exact facsimile of the original. Invisible nylon thread and a fine silk needle are recommended. The stitches then become nearly invisible (as used by the princess in Gulliver's Lilliputians), as three tucks are bound together at regular intervals after the fabric has been turned under with a strip of iron-on webbing. Since these curtains or draperies do not need to be drawn, fine small sequin pins (straight pins used for bead and sequin work) can be used (and hidden in the top pleats) to fasten the window covering to the wall.

Formal draperies, with a valance, can be made without taking in hand a needle or thread. The materials are gathered. Dye is used to alter the color of the textile, to subdue colors or minimize the contrast between design elements and the calico's white background.

The calico is dipped into biege dye. (Follow mixing directions on the package.)

Then the fabric is dipped into clear warm water and excess dye is rinsed out. The fabric is then pressed between sheets of paper toweling to set the color.

Pleats are formed by fusing narrow strips of fusible web (Stitch Witchery) . . .

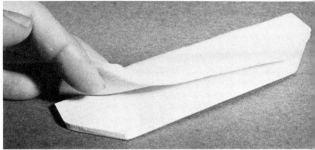

. . . with an iron set at medium heat. Small groups are done at one time.

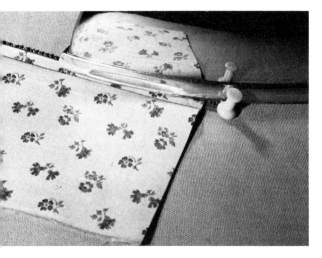

Rayon trim is also pressed into place using the fusible web.

A basswood valance and seat for the window are cut to shape. The seat is covered with a thin foam rubber padding.

Fabric is then covered around the wood parts and edges are glued to the back of the wood.

With trim added (using white glue), the parts are fixed permanently into place on the window. (This is the window shown in making a basic environment in Chapter 2.)

Dimity curtains by Elizabeth Scull.

A Victorian window arrangement by Elizabeth Scull.

A Victorian window treatment using cotton eyelet curtains. By Elizabeth Scull.

195

Reembroidered lace curtains and silk taffeta draperies by Elizabeth Scull.

Favorites of Colonial times were fabric wallpapers and matching Roman blinds, as well as hand-hooked rugs. *Courtesy: It's a Small World*

The golden bed and gossamer curtains are fit for a princess. Made by Agneta Domaczewicz.

Upholstery

A host of fabrics are available for upholstery, much as for curtains or draperies. Velour types such as mohair can be represented by plush knits and some velvets. Petit point in custom designs for a particular chair frame can also be made. Bargello is another highly adaptable canvas embroidery technique as illustrated here.

Upholstering a seat or couch is not necessarily performed as in upholstering an original, although for cutting fabric parts it is probably best to follow the original process. The upholstery base usually is different; it can be balsa wood carved to shape, foam rubber, or carved Styrofoam, to name a few. All of these base or stuffing materials can be pinned into to secure fabric while cutting, sewing, or gluing. One way of attaching upholstery to furniture is to tuck edges into thin grooves or cuts that have been sliced in the foam base and to glue edges; or it can be folded under and then glued to the underside of the base. Corners generally need to be mitered. Try to avoid overlapping of fabric. It usually creates out-of-scale lumping. Since there is no wear and tear on these fabrics, any shortcut, just so the final results look like a finished version, would work. This does not exclude, however, the possibility of following standard upholstering procedures, miniaturized.

197

A BARGELLO BENCH

Bargello is a very effective technique for making upholstery fabric. This is a bargello pattern for an upholstered
bench. The designer is Susan Richardson.

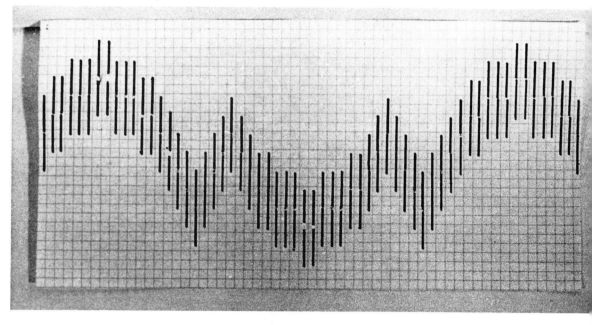

Materials are gathered. The mesh is
silk #38, the smallest mesh used for
petit point; and the thread is embroidery cotton.

The edge of the silk mesh is set with
water-diluted white glue. One cannot
use tape around the edges (as in full-
sized pieces) because the piece usually
is too small.

A bargello stitch is taken as shown in
the design diagram. Each stitch is four
spaces long.

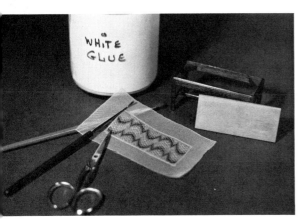

After the area is completed, materials are gathered for the upholstering operations.

No padding is used because the wood seat has been shaped. The folded silk mesh is glued in place around the wood seat. If the seat were not shaped, then a padding of foam rubber or cotton would help shape the surface.

The bench is by Paul A. Runyon.

Bargello-covered chairs by Elizabeth Scull.

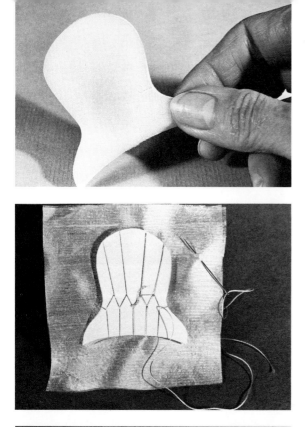

UPHOLSTERING A VICTORIAN CHAIR

The Victorian chair that was shown being made in Chapter 4 is now ready for upholstering. A pattern is cut from bristol board or oak tag 1/8 inch smaller than the chair back. Then it is padded on one side with a thin layer of foam rubber.

The fabric is also cut out larger all around than the pattern. Using silk thread, the tufting effect is created sewing straight through the pattern, foam, and fabric.

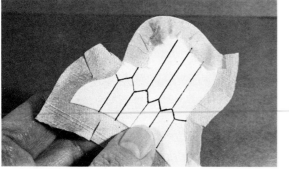

After sewing through the pattern, etc., excess fabric is clipped away leaving a 1/2-inch allowance all around. Edges are sliced so that when the fabric edges are glued to the pattern with white glue, they will not bunch.

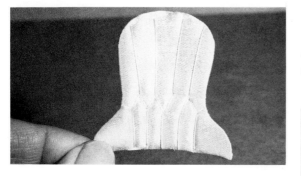

This is a unit for the top inside of the chair, ready for gluing.

White glue is used to hold the upholstered piece to the chair back. Hair clips provide just enough pressure. Golf ball elastic (from an unwrapped golf ball) can also be used by wrapping the upholstered parts with the elastic.

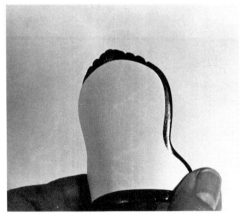

A bristol board pattern piece is also fitted for the back of the chair. This time no foam or tufting is necessary. The pattern is covered with fabric in the same manner as the front section and ...

... glued to the back.

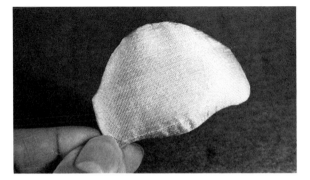

A 1/8 inch piece of basswood is covered with foam rubber to shape the seat (thicker in the center) and the seat is covered with fabric. Velverette is used to glue fabric in place. In order to pull the fabric tautly over the basswood, one part is glued and allowed to dry. Then the fabric is stretched, edges are slit, and the rest is adhered under the seat. (The completed chair can be seen as part of a Victorian parlor set in the color section.)

UPHOLSTERING A WING CHAIR

Upholstering a wing chair entails cutting fabric (this is woven ribbon) a bit larger for the front and then adhering the fabric to the chair with white glue (or Velverette).

Strips can be pieced if joined accurately.

A completed upholstered chair and all its component parts by Dolphin Originals.

Materials are gathered for making a petit point fire screen. (The incomplete screen is in the background on the right.)

A continental stitch is used with embroidery thread on #38 silk mesh.

In preparation for applying the petit point design, a paper pattern is cut to the exact size for the future fitting of the petit point.

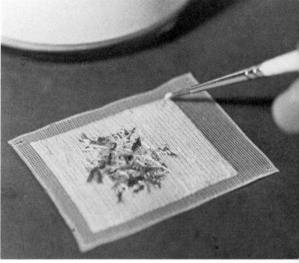

Edges around the petit point are sealed with white glue (which dries transparent) to keep the stitching from raveling when edges are trimmed.

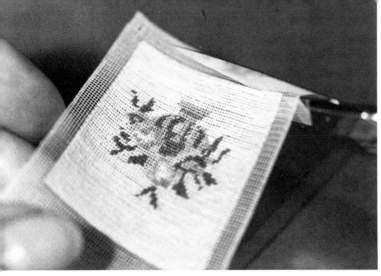

The petit point is cut to the size indicated by the paper pattern.

White glue is applied to the screen.

Then the petit point is pressed onto its backing with a dental tool.

The completed fire screen. The frame is by Paul A. Runyon.

Two other fire screens. These employ weavings from textiles.

A second-size William and Mary stool with turned legs and Spanish feet by S. A. Raube. The top is upholstered with a finely woven wool.

A tiny stool with petit point upholstery. Made by Elizabeth Scull.

Mahogany Chippendale chair by Paul A. Runyon and petit point upholstery.

Red leather wing chair by Chestnut Hill Studios.

MAKING A CHAIR WITH RUSH SEATING

A pattern is made and areas to be carved are drawn onto the 1/8-inch basswood. After carving details into the wood, the rest of the piece is cut out of the larger piece of wood and further refinements are made.

The back leg and upright support are traced on basswood from a pattern and cut out of the wood . . .

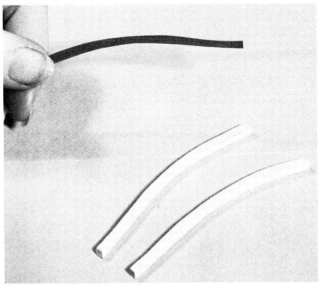

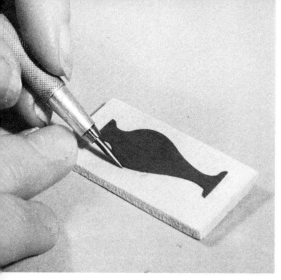

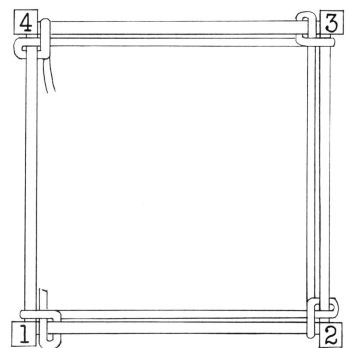

. . . so is the back to the chair. The front legs were turned earlier, as seen in Chapter 4. After parts were glued together, butt joint fashion, the chair is stained a mahogany color and varnished. The seating is to be made of rushwork.

This is a diagram that indicates the direction in which to repeat the winding of "rushing," starting from "1" and proceeding over and under to "2" then "3," and finally to "4." After "4" the operation is repeated until the seating area has been completely filled in. "Rushes" should be twisted in a direction away from the worker.

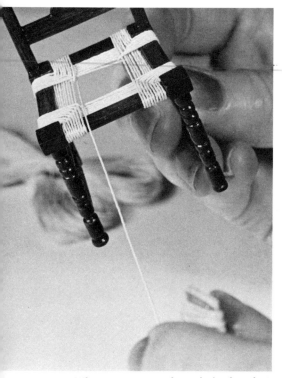

Each time the "rush" is looped around a chair seat part, it should be pulled tightly. The "rush" in this case, is extra fine linen rigging used in building ship models.

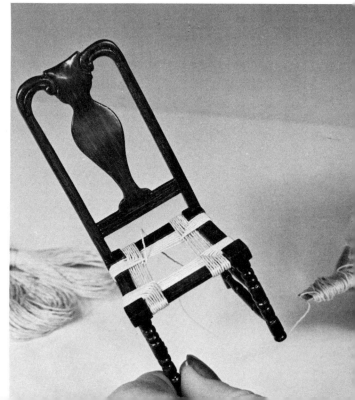

When you come to the end of a thread, tie the end underneath and tuck ends, burying them into the seat.

206

When one gets to this point, where there is no room for a bobbin wrapped with thread to be strung through, the thread length can be estimated and threaded through because it is stiff enough to be pushed through a small space.

The last bit of thread is knotted underneath and tucked in. The completed "rush" seat.

The completed chair.

A second-size antique Victorian rocker with a cane seat and back. *From the collection of Jeanne Knoop*

Two ladderback chairs with different seat patterns, similar
to rushwork, made in Columbia S.A.

WALLPAPERS—SELECTION AND MAKING

Selection

Wallpaper can be chosen over a broad range from standard commercial wallpapers printed in mini-patterns and textures to gift wrap papers, also with tiny patterns, to various textures of handmade and handblocked papers (often Japanese), some made for flyleaves of handbound books, and other papers sold in art supply stores. Old prints can also be used within wall panels for certain period rooms. Some can be hand-colored with pencils or watercolors. If the selection does not meet your needs, then you can design and make your own wallpaper.

Making Wallpaper

The base paper should be a finely textured, high-quality paper. Those used for charcoal drawing work well. They come in a variety of pastel-colored backgrounds, in enough of a range to meet most needs.

Starting with this background color, decide how the design is to be repeated—in stripes or columns, as alternating patterns arranged in bricklike repeats, as overall random spacing, or perhaps with the dominant element running in a diagonal pattern. Along with this is combined the design planning. Are you going to use more than one design

A selection of wallpapers especially made for minature rooms. (For sources, see "Supply Sources.")

element, perhaps with a dominant and a less important shape? And what colors do you require?

Design that considers purpose and period requirements, along with aspects of color, scale, repeat patterning, and subject matter, will help to determine the way the design will be reproduced.

Block printing, employing a pattern that has been cut into a piece of linoleum, wood, or even a rubber eraser, would work well. Even pin or nail heads and other found objects can be used. Stripes can be printed by coloring string and slapping it down on the paper. Brayers or other small rubber rollers can be carved into, or pieces of yarn, or cardboard can be glued onto the brayer to create a pattern. After the color has been rolled on the raised areas, the design will repeat itself as the brayer or roller is rolled along the page. Several designs can be overlapped, perhaps each in a different color.

Silk screening is another technique but it requires a good deal of skill. In this case, a resist of some type—liquid, cut paper, or photo—is placed on a silk screen. The screen is placed over the paper and with a squeegee, ink is drawn evenly over the masked screen. When the screen is lifted off the paper, a positive design is registered. Many colors can be coordinated with this. Each design that is overlayed usually has a different screen.

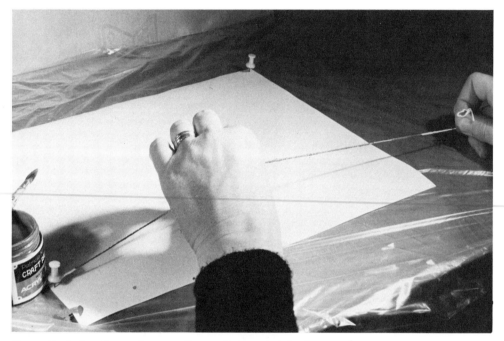

One method of making one's own wallpaper designs. A string is covered with paint, held tautly, and slapped onto the paper, leaving a stripe.

"Found" objects can be used as well. Here a nail head is coated using a sponge and paint as an improvised stamp pad, and then the head of the nail, charged with color, is pressed onto the background. A soft padding under the printing surface helps make for more precise impressions.

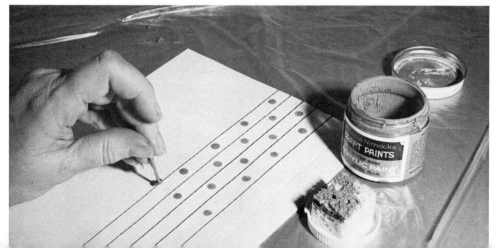

Stencils can also be cut into waxy heavy paper or architects' linen. Then with a stippling technique, using a flat-bottomed, stiff brush (stencil brush), paint is thinly applied over the openings. After the stencil has been lifted away, a positive is left. This image can be repeated and colors can be added or changed.

Printing requires a positive and ink or paint (acrylic is fine) to be transferred with even pressure on the proper background space. Try your design on scrap paper first.

Flocked paper can be made by running thin threads of white glue in the desired design on the paper and then dusting the flocking over it. After the glue has dried, shake off the excess flocking.

A very elegant and expensive way of creating wallpaper is to use a favorite full-sized design and have it reduced and printed by a printer.

A subdued scenic wallpaper is used in this Colonial American room by Frederick Hicks. Where there is difficulty in matching patterns, it is best to use wall moldings as a frame around the wallpaper pattern. *Courtesy: Frederick Hicks*

A Colonial American bedroom with areas papered and paneled. *Courtesy: Frederick Hicks*

6 | FORMING ACCESSORIES USING GLASS, CERAMICS, PLASTICS, PLASTER, AND METAL

It has always been a tour de force for craftsmen to replicate their craft in the smallest possible size with exact duplication of detail. It still is an achievement because precision is a challenge. One can "get away with" an imperfection on a large form that would be completely unacceptable in miniature. The charm of any miniature environment is, more than any other aspect, in the exactness of its accessories—objects of glass, ceramics, metal, plastics, plaster, and wood. The challenge is here too, if one considers that a six-inch pen translates to one-half inch, and yet the pen, in order to be identifiable, should be complete in every detail. Imagine, too, weaving a basket that is only one-half inch high and five-eighths inch in diameter! Yet, the feat of throwing a miniscule pot or blowing a tiny decanter is what dramatizes the achievement of creating a miniature environment.

It would take a very rare person to be accomplished in all the skills used to make accessories, and explaining all the how-to details here would turn this book into a series of books; therefore, just highlights are given, some more detailed in process than others. Whether one endeavors to create accessories from scratch, improvising and adapting pieces or buying objects from specialists, knowing something about the

212

An ever-so-tiny pen with a metal pen point.

processes helps in understanding what to look for when selecting a ready-made accessory.

ABOUT GLASSBLOWING

Glass, usually transparent or translucent, is a supercooled liquid consisting of selenium or (the most commonly used) pure oxide such as silica, added to more complicated mixtures. These substances have to be melted at high temperatures to create the glass material. Glass, surprisingly, has no definite melting point, but rather it has a softening range. Heating glass even at low temperatures tends to soften it, although it may not be visually evident.

A glass commonly used by glassblowers is Corning glass #7740. Its working temperature is at 1220°C and its softening point is at 820°C. After the glass form has been blown and shaped (if it is large), it must be annealed to relieve strains and reduce the possibility for breakage. The annealing temperature for this brand of glass is 555°C.

Glassblowing equipment can vary from the simple to the complex. What one chooses depends, of course, upon one's involvement. Essentially, a Bunsen burner is the most common heat source for glassblowers. Glassblower's goggles, tweezers, marking pencils, carbon paddles, carbon rods, asbestos cloth, and carborundum are other necessities. With these special materials, one can form mini-glass forms.

Before beginning, it is best to keep in mind these basic concepts:

pulling the glass decreases the diameter and wall thickness,

blowing the glass increases the diameter and decreases the wall thickness,

heating the glass decreases the diameter and increases the wall thickness,

and pushing an enlarged tube increases the diameter and wall thickness.

The working point of glass is the temperature at which the glass is most malleable. When a rod of glass is introduced to a flame, the glass begins to flow, with gravity doing much of the work. That is why the glassblower has to keep the glass continually turning; otherwise, glass will drop off. The glass should be turned in the direction that one wants it to flow, and the form has to be turned all the time.

Since the initial glass tube is hollow, blowing is accomplished by placing the tube in the mouth (it doesn't burn lips because glass doesn't

GLASS BLOWING WITH DAVID DORSI

The end of a (#7740) Corning Glass tube is melted with the heat of a gas/oxygen flame.

After removing the tube from the flame, and the glass is soft enough, gravity does most of the work as the glass flows. That is why you have to keep twisting the glass between your fingers, otherwise the flowing glass will drop off. (It should be turned in the direction that you want it to flow.)

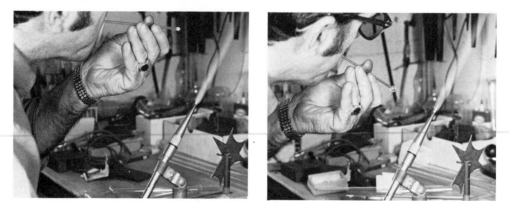

While the glass tube is hot, blow through the tube. If long enough, and you can hold it, it won't burn your lips. The blowing force you use depends upon how hot the glass is. The cooler the glass gets, the more blowing force needed.

The minute the glass cools (but not all the way) and begins to set up, place it into the flame.

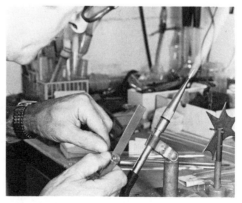

After the ball has been blown, cut it off with a smooth Nickelson file, or any second-cut file. Break the glass rod off the ball. (The ball is cooler at that point.)

Attach a hot glass rod to the base of the ball, holding the neck with a tweezers.

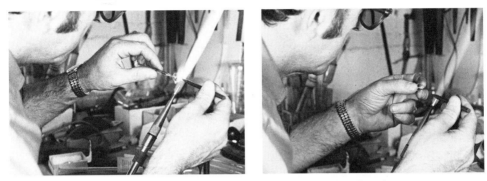

With a small pointed carbon rod used as a flaring tool, revolve the rod in the tube to open the tube end of the glass ball into a flared funnellike shape. To flatten the bottom of the ball, holding it around the neck, reheat it to the softening point and flatten it with a carbon paddle by pressing the paddle against the bottom of the ball.

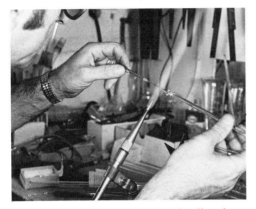

To make the stopper, heat a rod and pull or draw out the rod to taper it.

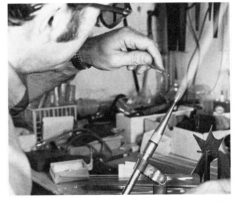

Gather a ball at the end by placing the rod back in the fire, turning it all the time.

Use a flat carbon paddle to shape the stopper. Break off the stopper with a file. After the edge is cut away, place it back in the flame to fire-polish it.

To fit stopper in flask, use #400 carborundum abrasive powder mixed with water into a liquid. Place some on stopper end and neck of the bottle and at the same time rotate the two, stopper in neck, until they fit.

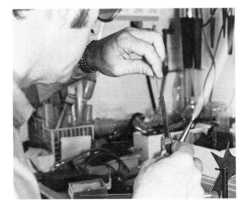

A completed glass flask with stopper, all of one inch tall. By David Dorsi.

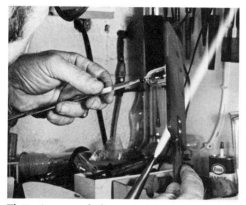

Flattening an end of a vase with a carbon paddle.

Flaring a vase with a flaring rod.

A tiny pitcher by David Dorsi.

Two flasks by David Dorsi.

A blown glass chandelier by David Dorsi.

conduct heat). The heat of glass determines how much blowing force is needed; therefore, the cooler the glass gets, the more force is needed.

The minute glass begins to cool, it begins to set up. While working this type of glass, the material should not be allowed to cool below 550°C, else strains will appear. Below 820°C, this glass is no longer formable.

In creating a miniature vessel the large shapes are formed first, such

A crystal miniature decanter from England.

An assortment of miniature glass and ceramic forms from the collection of Elizabeth Scull.

as blowing a ball, then this is cut off with a smooth Nickelson file, or any second cut file. The basic shape can be attached at the base end with the point of another rod to hold the ball temporarily and permit it to be rotated and maneuvered. Then a small pointed carbon rod is used as a flaring tool to open the tube at the neck section into a flared, funnel-like shape.

After this, the glass can then be held with a tweezers as it cools below softening, and the glass rod then is snapped away from the ball. Next, the ball is brought up to forming point again and the base is flattened with a carbon paddle.

A stopper can be made by tapering a rod by applying a pulling force to both ends and shaping it with a flat carbon paddle. The stopper is then broken off by marking the glass at the proper point with a file. After the form has been cut away, the piece is returned to the flame to allow the fire to flame polish the raw edges.

In order to create a frosted end on the stopper, a mixture of #400 carborundum abrasive powder is stirred with water until it is liquid. This is applied to the end of the stopper and, with its carborundum coating, is placed into the bottle neck and rotated until it fits the bottle's neck.

When objects are very small, there usually is no reason to anneal them. But if annealing is necessary, the entire piece is usually heated uniformly (and allowed to cool uniformly) in an oven. After the glass reaches a soft orange flame color, the annealing temperature is gradually reduced until the form is cool.

ABOUT CERAMIC FORM-MAKING

Clay is a natural product that comes from the earth and is the world's most plentiful resource, after water. But the clay body one uses for making ceramic forms most often has been formulated by processors who remove impurities and mix different kinds of clay together, sometimes with other ingredients, to achieve special clay body properties. For miniature forms, it usually is best to acquire a smooth clay body that matures at a low temperature. (Firing makes the clay harder and denser.) The advantage of firing clay at lower temperatures is that it permits the use of brightly colored glazes, which would burn out at high temperatures. Prepared clay is ready to use, has the proper consistency, and ease of manipulating. Debra McKnight, on the other hand, uses a stoneware body and fires her pots at high temperatures, which helps to reduce the size of her pieces. She also uses higher fire natural-colored stoneware-type glazes.

The firing temperature of clay usually is indicated as its maturing temperature with nomenclature such as "Cone 04" which means the point of a cone will bend at cone 04 heat which is 1940°F or 1060°C. This is the middle range of earthenware firing temperature. Stoneware, on the other hand, is fired at at least cone 8 or 1260°C. Firing at high temperatures though is not necessary for makers of miniature pots.

Shaping Clay

After the clay is purchased, one can play around with ways of manipulating a small lump to create an object. There are many ways of forming clay into vessels. Pinching the clay into shape with fingers is one way. Another is rolling it out into an even thickness between two parallel sticks that act as thickness guides for a rolling pin that rolls on the two tracks. The lump of clay which has been placed between the sticks can be rolled then into an even flatness. When a piece of uniform thickness has been formed, using a knife, shapes can be cut and these pieces can be attached together to create forms. Clay joints have to be blended so no cracks or spaces are visible.

Tiny lumps can also be rolled into snakelike rope and then in a coiling fashion built up into a shape. Each coil should be adhered solidly to the pieces that adjoin it. Coil and slab work can be combined as well. Clay can also be pressed or poured into a plaster mold. When pressed into a mold, a slablike shape is usually used and when poured, the clay is mixed with water until it is a heavy pourable liquid called a "slip." The (at least) two-part plaster mold, held together with a heavy rubber band, absorbs the liquid, leaving a deposit of clay on the walls of the plaster mold. When the water evaporates, the clay becomes leather-hard and shrinks away from the walls, making the miniature part easy to release. Clay forms can be trimmed with knives or tautly held thin wire.

Throwing a pot requires the most skill. A wide range of shapes can be made with forms later shaped with tool or hand to vary the basic symmetrical contour that comes off the wheel. Lips are made for pitchers, and handles are added using threadlike bits of clay. A series of photos describes how Debra McKnight throws a tiny pot. Most ceramists who have mastered the turning art can make miniatures. They often do it for fun.

THROWING MINIATURE CLAY
FORMS WITH DEBORAH
MCKNIGHT

After the clay has been prepared, a larger lump of clay is centered on an electric wheel (a kick wheel can also be used).

Then a smaller lump is demarcated on the top. With forefinger and thumb, the center is opened.

At this point, with gentle pressure, the form is shaped at bottom and squeezed in at the top. Because the form is too small at this point to place a finger inside the piece, to counteract outside pressure, sculpture tools or brush handles are used on inside portions.

When the form has been shaped, it is removed by pulling a fine taut piece of wire through the clay at the base of the wheel.

The reverse end of a paint brush helps to shape the pouring spout . . .

... a pinch between forefinger and thumb completes the form.

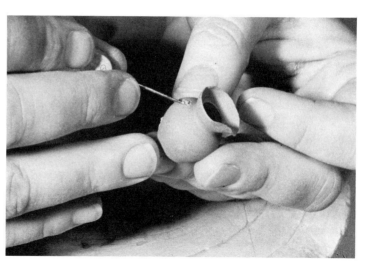

The tiny pitcher is then placed on a plaster bat until leather-hard and ready for trimming and the addition of a handle. The spots where the handle is to be placed are roughened with a pin tool and slip (water and clay mixture) is placed on those areas.

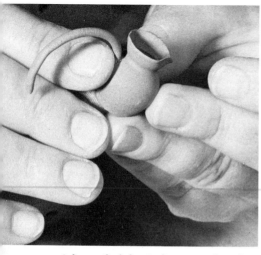

A fine coil of clay is then pressed on those two spots and edges are smoothed.

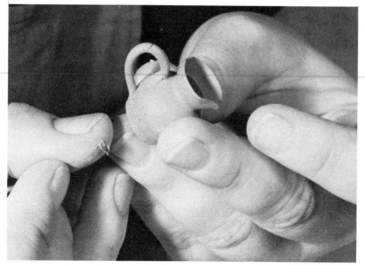

Excess is trimmed away and a handle is formed.

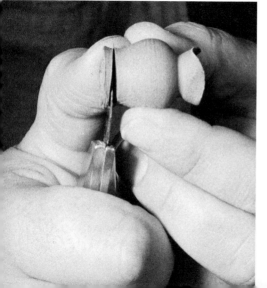

Using a utility knife, excess clay is trimmed from the bottom.

After a first firing (bisque firing), decoration is applied with underglaze and then the entire piece is overglazed. The piece is fired from between 1800°F to 2400°F, appropriate for that glaze.

The completed pitcher, 7/8 inch, by Deborah McKnight.

FORMING A SMALL VASE

Forming a small vase requires the same beginning preparation. Index finger, middle finger, and thumb do most of the forming while the wheel is turning.

Gradually the widest part is flared outward, as the wheel continues to turn ...

... the top is pulled in to close the opening somewhat. Note how her thumb is controlling the shape.

223

At this point, a tool is necessary to shape the lip . . .

. . . with a final delicate touch of pressure on top . . .

. . . the shape is formed. A wooden coffee stirrer is used to refine the surface. The form is removed with the tautly pulled wire and is placed on a plaster bat to dry.

"The Pottery" by Deborah McKnight. The pots range from 1/2 inch to one inch tall.

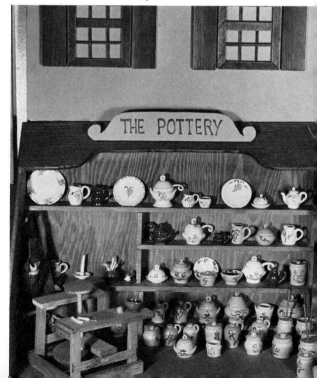

Another "Pottery" by Deborah McKnight showing a scaled-down version of the potter's wheel.

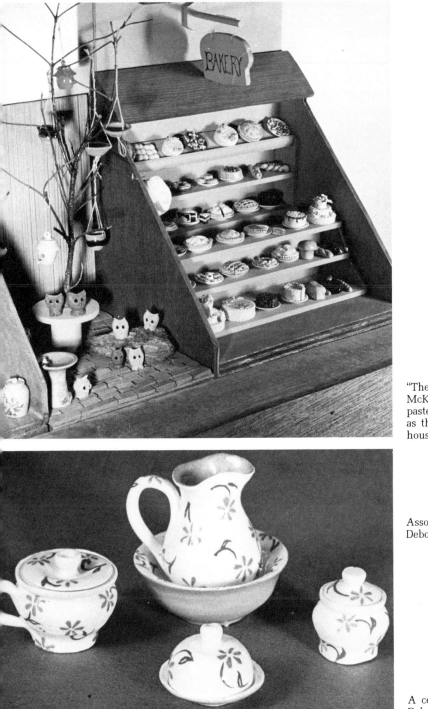

"The Bakery" by Deborah McKnight. The cakes and pasteries are ceramic, as well as the owls, furniture, bird-houses, and bricks.

Assorted ceramic forms by Deborah McKnight.

A ceramic bathroom set by Deborah McKnight.

DECORATING CLAY AT THIS POINT

Dental tools can be used to press fine textures into the clay just before it is leather-hard. Some minerals also can be painted on at that stage as well. These will mix with the glaze (which consists of finely ground glass oxides and minerals suspended in water) to become colored decoration that is an integral part of the ceramics. Decorating with minerals, tools, and glazes has to be done very finely in order to approximate design proportions.

Drying and Firing Clay Forms

Plaster of Paris (U.S. Gypsum Co. pottery plaster or use Red Top) is useful to the potter. Plaster's water-absorbing properties help clay to dry out. Note that the part nearest the plaster will dry out faster. (Clay that dries evenly is less apt to crack.) Plaster bats, formed by pouring plaster into pie pans, also make useful working areas and are portable for moving the clay forms from working to drying areas.

After the clay form has dried to the point when it contains no water (to the touch), pieces (without glaze) are stacked in a kiln and fired to maturing temperature. Moisture left in clay can cause pieces to explode when fired.

There are many types of kilns. A simple type can be made of insulating refractory bricks, stacked into a cubelike box on a brick stand, with four holes at the bottom left for the flames of four Bunsen burners, and an opening at the top (for inserting and stacking pieces) which can be closed by laying two bricks over it. A layer of asbestos millboard fastened with a ring of iron rods can enclose the whole kiln and hold the bricks together. This kiln can be fired at least to cone 04. But kilns also come in various sizes and complexities, all the way to giant walk-in versions. The homemade variety indicated here or a small test-sized kiln heated with electric coils (like those on a hot plate) is adequate for miniature work.

Unglazed greenware, dried, unfired clay forms, can be stacked closely, even one piece inside another. After stacking and firing to the proper cone temperature, the kiln heat source is turned off and allowed to cool off. When the tip of the proper temperature cone (which is placed in the kiln so that it remains visible) melts and curls downward, it is time to remove or cut off the heat source. After the first firing, these pieces are called *bisque ware* and are ready for glazing. After pieces are glazed, they must be fired once again so that the glazed surface (which now is a suspended glass powder) will melt and fuse to the clay body. Glazed pieces, however, when stacked in a kiln, must be placed on ceramic stilts to keep them from becoming attached to the kiln shelf later, and must *not* touch other pieces while in the kiln. When the glaze is heated it liquefies and, after cooling, forms into the hard, glasslike surface with which we are so familiar. If parts touch, therefore, they will fuse together upon cooling.

Glaze firing heat varies according to the chemical composition of the glaze. This is indicated on the package upon purchase or built in when formulated.

Glazes

One could write several books on glazes alone. The chemical aspects are quite involved. A glaze is basically made of glass-forming oxides and sometimes, with the aid of fluxes, liquefies at high heat. Glazes are formulated to relate to the maturing temperatures of clays and are fired at the same cone points, such as cone 04 for some earthenware. Prepared glazes with standardized and pretested colors indicated for particular cone firings can be purchased in hobby and ceramic supply stores. It is probably best to start with prepared glazes, particularly when working with very small pieces.

Glazes are applied while liquid by dipping the bisque ware into the liquid glaze or by brushing an even layer (if evenness is desired) onto the clay, using a soft brush such as camel's hair or sable. Keep the glaze off the underpart of your piece. A coating of wax on the base will keep the glaze from sticking. Wax can also be used as a resist material to paint designs on the pot. Wherever the wax is placed, the glaze (which is water-based) will not stick. The glaze should dry completely before firing in the kiln.

Glazes can also be mixed together and pieces, once fired, can be re-covered with glazes and fired again.

Just as in firing greenware (unfired clay), when the proper temperature cone melts and curls downward, the heat source should be shut off. The kiln should be allowed to cool completely before removing glazed pieces. If you find that glaze has dripped on the underpart of the piece, you can grind it away with a carborundum stone and water or with a file.

Three versions of the same ceramic form from Chinautla, Guatemala. The largest one is about 4 inches tall, the middle-sized one is one inch, and the one on the man's back is 1/4 inch.

One-inch ceramic forms from Honduras.

Tiny American Indian forms from The House of Miniatures. On the left is a Jemez plate, next are two Hopi bowls,
and, on the right, a rare San Ildefonso miniature plate
(Santa Fe, New Mexico). *Courtesy: The House of Miniatures*

A garden seat and lavabo from the Ginger Jar.

Blue onion (design) tea set by Ellen Krucker Blauer
of the Peddlers Shop.

Two Acama Indian pots and a Hopi canteen from The House of Miniatures. *Courtesy: The House of Miniatures*

Ceramic tea set from Chestnut Hill Studio.

Ceramic sculptures 1 inch tall from England.

Staffordshire figures 1/2 inch tall.

Miniature Victorian what-not shelves by Elizabeth Scull, and a collection of ceramic miniatures.

ABOUT WORKING WITH PLASTICS

Plastic is a huge field consisting of thousands of different kinds of man-made materials. The potential of using plastics is vast, and so are its possibilities for the miniature maker. Processes here, too, can fill many volumes.* Some of the potential uses, such as working with acrylics and foams, have been covered earlier in this book. In this section, molding tiny forms using a two-part epoxy putty, squeezing flowers out of a tube containing silicone, making RTV silicone molds and then casting glasslike and metal-like shapes in the molds with polyester and epoxy, or forming a stained glass window of polyester resin, as well as heat fusing transparent, fusible plastics into beads and glasslike forms, will be illustrated and described.

RTV Silicone Caulking Material

Flower forms can be made of bread-dough mixtures, plaster, re-melted polyethylene, clay, paper, and a host of materials. Most of these materials require molding or modeling to form the flowers, but by using an RTV silicone caulking material, flower forms can be literally squeezed from a tube. The advantage to using silicone is that the form

*Coauthor Thelma Newman has written four texts and many articles just on the subject of plastics.

230

is flexible and the surface is much like a plant texture. The tube of silicone can be purchased in any building supply, paint, or hardware store. It comes in many colors and is usually used as a bathtub caulking compound.

We use clear RTV silicone and mix it with powdered or acrylic colors. Flower forms also can be painted afterwards with acrylic artist colors. Wax paper is a good base because the silicone can be peeled away easily, otherwise it sticks rather tenaciously to whatever it is squeezed on.

By shaping out of fine wire a stem and central spines for leaves, the colored silicone can be coated over the wire. Flower and leaf parts are modeled with dental tools, applicator sticks, toothpicks, or knives. After the silicone hardens to its final rubbery, flexible texture in a few hours, edges can be trimmed with a scissors. Cuticle or decoupage scissors are good tools for cutting fine contours. The leaves can be shaped by bending the wire skeleton.

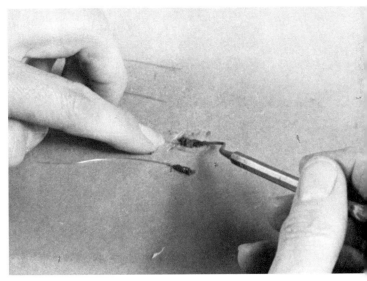

Silicone (RTV) caulking material can be mixed with color (powdered or acrylic) and squeezed out on a piece of wax paper over a fine wire armature to create floral forms.

Fine instruments (such as dental tools) can refine and texture shapes.

The material dries within an hour and can be trimmed with a knife or scissors.

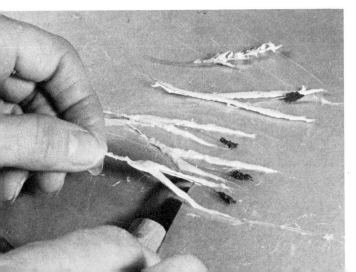
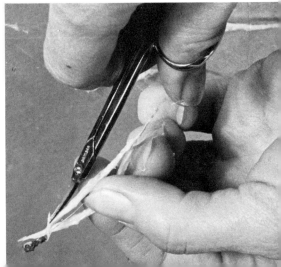

An arrangement of RTV silicone
flowers two inches tall.

Epoxy Putty

Another building supply or hardware store item is the two-part
epoxy putties consisting of a filled epoxy base and a catalyst. By knead-
ing equal amounts of the two bricks that are packaged (in several colors)
into a homogeneous, puttylike consistency, any number of items can be
shaped. The material hardens in about an hour into a stone-hard substance. Flowers, fruit, vegetables, bread, pottery, and the like can be
formed by rolling, coiling, squeezing, pinching, flattening, and otherwise finely shaping the epoxy putty with dental tools.

The final shape, after hardening, can then be painted with oil-based
or acrylic paints.

Materials for forming flowers
from two-part epoxy.

Two equal parts of epoxy are kneaded together until
thoroughly mixed. It is puttylike in consistency.

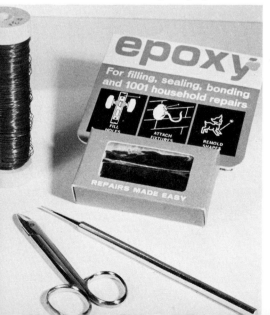

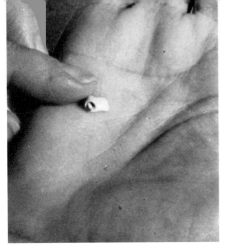

Small pieces are flattened and then rolled into rosebudlike shapes.

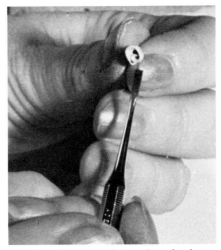

Dental tools are used to refine the forms. Wire is placed into the bud and the base of the flower is squeezed to fit tightly around the wire.

After hardening, the roses were painted with acrylic and sprayed later with Krylon to impart a glaze. Dried leaves are placed in the arrangement. The vase is the one turned from a spool shown earlier in Chapter 4. It had been painted with acrylic, and metal paper embossing (decoupage trim) was glued around the base and rim.

Fusible Crystals or Pellets

Crystallike pellets sold under various brand names, such as Dec-ets or Cookin' Crystals, can be melted and fused on cookie sheets or in mold forms into glasslike textures. Individual crystals, when melted on an aluminum cookie sheet under any heat source (we use a portable broiler oven) at 350°–400°F, will soften to a moldable consistency. At that point the crystals fuse and can be shaped using tweezers, spatulas, and other wooden or metal tools, or the crystals can be penetrated with wire. Upon cooling, the plastic will harden. But it also can be remelted and reshaped any number of times. Even cutaway scraps can be reused.

Final shapes can be sanded, sawed, drilled, and polished, using wood cutting tools and metal polishing buffing wheels and supplies. Aluminum, Pyrex, and glazed stoneware make for the best molds because they can withstand heat and their surfaces act as a release agent, allowing the cooled plastic to come away from the surface. Do not, however, use molds with undercuts, where the hardened plastic will lock into place and would require breaking or resoftening to be released.

These crystals can be water clear and also come in many transparent, translucent, and opaque colors. They can be purchased in art supply and hobby shops and catalogs, or from the specific supplier indicated in the "Supply Sources" section of this book.

Fusible, clear plastic pellets (Dec-Ets or Cookin' Crystals) are placed separately on an aluminum cookie sheet.

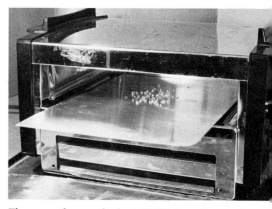

They are then melted at 350°F. to soften and round the edges of each pellet . . .

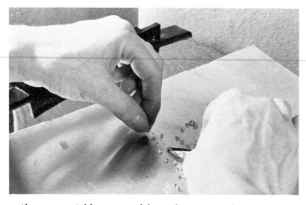

. . . they are quickly removed from the oven so that a wire can be inserted in the softened plastic. As the wire is pressed into the crystal, a tweezers helps to squeeze one end producing a teardrop effect.

These crystals are then hung on a jewelry finding that becomes a Victorian candlestick. Crystals can also be used to make chandeliers.

MAKING A BOWL

Using an aluminum jello mold as a mold form for making a bowl, fusible plastic pellets are poured into the cavity . . .

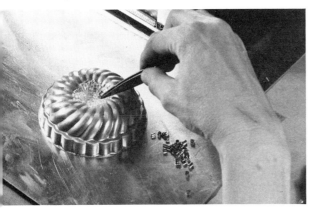

. . . pressed and placed along the sides so that about two layers of crystals line the shape.

The form is heated until the pellets fuse.

Any places where there are spaces, the plastic is pressed together. More crystals can be added and reheated, any number of times.

The plastic quickly cools (and can be dropped into cold water), and then separates from the mold.

The bottom of the form can be flattened by pressing it on the top of the hot oven.

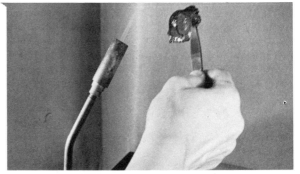

Edges can be softened by quickly revolving the shape through the flame of a propane torch.

The completed shape.

Liquid Plastic Solder and Polyester Resin

A heatless, fast-setting silverlike liquid solder that can be squeezed from a tube (and purchased in hardware stores) can be used to make the cames or metal dividing areas for stained glass windows, as well as a host of small metal shapes. The material when hardened has little dimensional stability, therefore it requires the support of something else to hold its shape. But for the stained glass window, or tiny metal forms, it functions beautifully.

Polyester resin, a two-part syrupy plastic, that can be colored with transparent to opaque dyes, hardens into a glasslike substance. The two parts have to be weighed or measured and mixed according to the manufacturer's indicated formula. After a thorough stirring with a wooden stirrer or tongue depressor, the mixture (which usually is colored with dyes) can be poured into molds or into spaces defined by the raised solder lines, as in the stained glass window illustrated here. After about one hour, the polyester will harden into a rigid material much like glass.

One aspect of which to be aware, particularly if the manufacturer provides only scanty instruction, is that the catalyst, a peroxide, requires careful handling. Don't get it on your skin and don't inhale it. Use ventilation when using polyester to remove the fumes. Also, a technical aspect of concern is that when thin sections are poured, more catalyst is required to induce hardening. Conversely, thicker castings require less catalyst. Catalyst is used in *proportion to the quantity, weight, or thickness.* Too much catalyst mixed in a thick casting will cause the plastic to smoke because heat is generated by the catalyst in the curing or hardening process.

Wax, silicone, Mylar, polyvinyl alcohol, and polyethylene are good release agents. Polyester resin will stick to almost anything else. The stained glass window was made on a piece of Mylar.

Polyester resin is a wonderful material with great versatility and possibilities once you learn how to handle it and understand its properties and potentials.

236

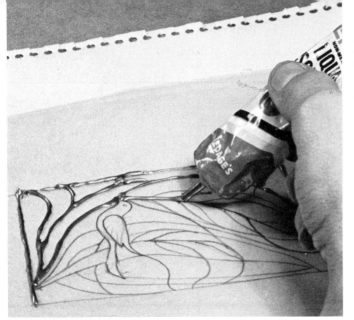

MAKING A STAINED GLASS (PLASTIC) WINDOW

Lepage's Liquid Solder forms just the correct bead of "metal" to contain a glasslike pouring of polyester resin. The solder is drawn in a bead on a clear Mylar sheet (wax paper can be used as well), following the outlines of the original drawing (which is under the Mylar).

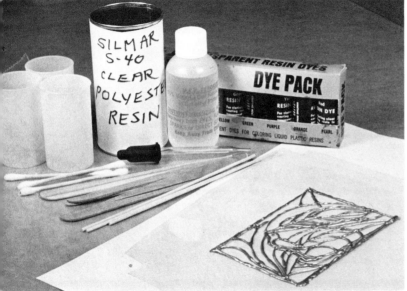

When the outline has hardened (in about an hour), materials for coloring and pouring the polyester resin are readied.

Small amounts of polyester resin are mixed in a mixing container with color, stirred well and ...

... then catalyst (MEK peroxide) is added by the drop and stirred very thoroughly. At this point, it is ready to be delivered with an eyedropper to the approximate space of the window.

A cotton swab is used for cleanup wherever there is an overflow.

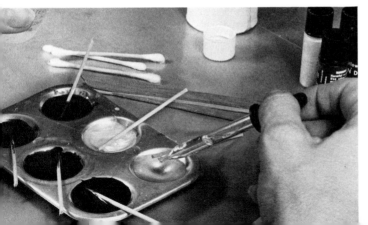

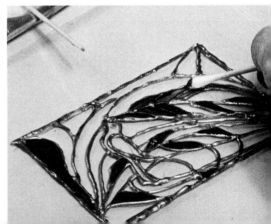

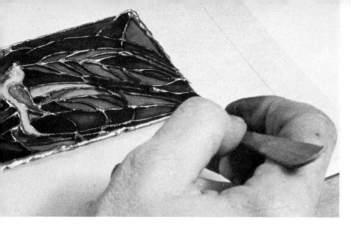

An extra bead of liquid solder is run around the outside and then molded with a tongue depressor.

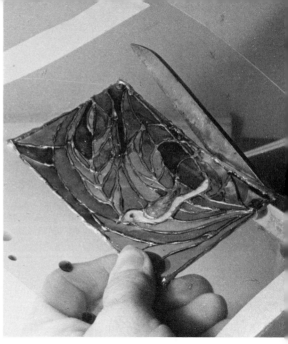

The resin cures within two to three hours. It can be pulled away from the backing or, because the Mylar can provide some support, trimmed with a scissors.

The completed window.

RTV Silicone Moldmaking and Casting with Epoxy and Polyester Resins

Using a vase, spoon or other implement, bowl, chess piece, sculpture, and so on made of any hard material including clay or wax, a flexible, room-temperature vulcanizing (hence, RTV) silicone mold can be made. One simply mixes two parts together according to the manufacturer's recommendations, and pours it around the form. The silicone hardens to a rubbery consistency overnight. Then the original form is pried out and the mold is ready to receive a casting material such as epoxy or polyester. Since silicone acts as a release agent, the mold need not be coated, and hundreds of pieces can be produced in it.

The usual considerations have to be observed, as in any moldmaking procedure, namely, a rigid container has to be found or made to contain the original. If the original piece has cavities, they have to be filled. Areas like handles have to be covered or filled as well, or else the mold material, when it is poured, will lock through the handle or hole. Slight undercuts are okay because the silicone is flexible enough to pull away and allow the release of the positive, but severe undercutting would require making a two-part mold. Accommodation also has to be made for a hole in which to pour the casting resin and for the exit of air. It is possible, when casting in a mold, to trap air, particularly in bottom corners. The result is a hole or pit, marring the complete form. To avoid this, sprues or vents in the shape of a funnel or tube should be attached with clay or wax to the original. The original then is placed upside down or rightside up in the mold container before pouring the RTV silicone around it, so that eventually the pouring spout and venting channel are exposed for use. Certainly, these parts should not be buried under mold material. But they can be attached to the bottom of the mold box, so that the silicone does not seep underneath and mask the opening.

These sprues, vents, and cavity fillers can be cut or ground away after the hardened plastic resin part is removed from the mold. Rough areas are then sanded and polished. The final piece should replicate, exactly, to the finest detail, the positive. RTV silicone is one of the best mold materials available, mainly because of its ease of handling as well as its perfection in copying every detail of the original.

Polyester resin and epoxy can be mixed with their respective catalysts according to the manufacturer's directions, colored or filled with metal, sand, or other fillers to impart color and texture, and then poured into the sprue or funnel part of the mold. When mixing the resins with their color (which should be done first) and then the catalyst, try not to introduce air bubbles. If there are bubbles, allow the catalyzed resin to sit for a few moments to allow bubbles to rise to the top and pop. (You will have a working time of about one-half hour.)

This holds true when mixing the RTV silicone as well. One technique, when pouring the RTV silicone, is to pour aiming at a corner of the mold container and allow the silicone to flow around and over the form so bubbles are less apt to get trapped around the original. Also, if bubbles are contained in the RTV silicone mixture, pouring from a height of about one foot, so that the streaming of silicone is stretched into a thin pouring, helps to "stretch out" the trapped air bubbles. Do not plop the resin into the mold container in one fast pour. Your result will probably be full of unvented cavities and pitholes. When care is taken, your result will be as good as the original.

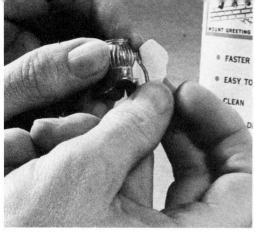

MAKING AN RTV SILICONE MOLD

A miniature positive model of whatever you want to cast can be made from scratch out of any kind of material; an antique or other model can be made as well. Plasti-Tak is used here to temporarily plug up holes and cavities. (The Plasti-Tak pulls away later without marring the original.)

A small box is readied to receive the forms. And then the pieces are rubber cemented to the base of the box to temporarily keep the tiny pieces from moving around and to prevent the rubber mold material from oozing underneath. This glued-down area will later become the pouring entrance.

Two items, a glass bottle and metal pitcher, are attached to the base of the handmade box with just enough space around them to be encased in rubber.

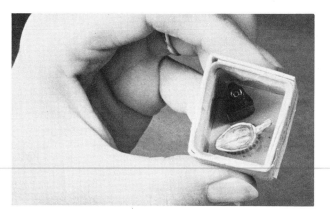

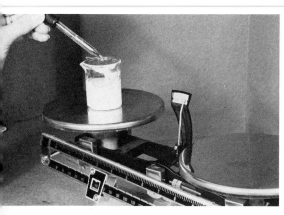

The RTV silicone is weighed and catalyst is added and weighed as well, following the manufacturer's directions.

Catalyst and silicone are mixed thoroughly, without introducing air in the stirring process, . . .

. . . and then poured in a thin stream into the box, aiming at one corner. The forms will be covered to at least 1/8 inch to 1/4 inch above their edges.

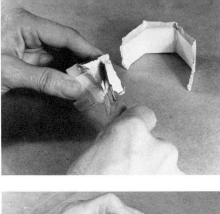

After the RTV silicone cures overnight, the box is cut away from the mold.

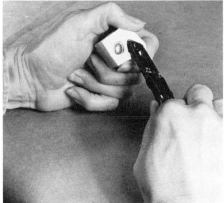

Then, with pliers, the originals are pulled out. (This was the bottom of the mold.)

At this point the mold is ready for filling. A clear epoxy is going to be used to make a casting that will look like glass. Here the epoxy resin is being weighed following proportions indicated by the manufacturer.

The proper weight of catalyst is added to the resin and . . .

. . . both are mixed thoroughly.

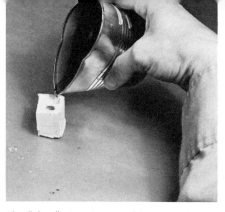

The "glass" piece is poured first.

Then, a metal (aluminum) powder is mixed with the remaining epoxy.

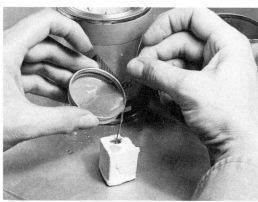

The metal mixture is poured into the cavity of the little pitcher.

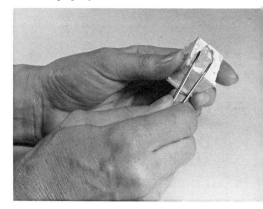

When cured, in several hours, both pieces are removed from the flexible mold.

The completed pitcher.

The base of the glass flask needs some refining. It is being ground flat on a grinding wheel in a Dremel Moto-Tool.

242

The completed castings. Several hundred can be made.

Polyester resin and catalyst are weighed, mixed, and colored.

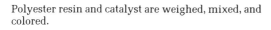

The hardened resin plate is removed.

MAKING A SMALL PLATE MOLD

A similar procedure is used to make a mold of a small plate. Here the plate has been removed from the mold and the back trimmed.

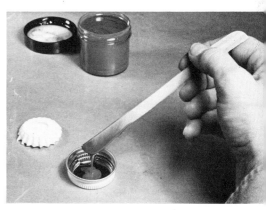

The mixture is poured to slightly over-flowing above the mold line. (Polyester resin will shrink a bit upon curing.)

Any repairs and refinements are made by sanding . . .

. . . or buffing with a muslin or felt buff at low speeds.

And the plates may be left as is, or further finished, as a gilded plate using gold Rub n Buff.

WORKING WITH PLASTER

Plaster, for most applications, is molded, but plaster can be coated over a form using a spatula or cast into a block and carved with knives or motorized drill bits.

The RTV silicone mold described earlier can be used or rubber molds can be made as well. The rubber mold is very flexible and requires use of a release such as petroleum jelly or green soap to keep the plaster from sticking.

Plaster can then be gilded or painted with any kind of paint in a variety of finishes. As a material, plaster is a very inexpensive substance to use for making ornaments, fruit, vegetable, bread and cake forms, lamp bases, sculptures, wall sconces, and even some furniture parts. Plaster is not strong enough, however, to be cast in very thin sections. The epoxies would be the strongest of the molding or casting materials.

Mixing Plaster

Except for plastic and plaster mixtures such as Hydrocal, most plasters are made of gypsum rock. Gypsum has an affinity for water, and when mixed with water it sets into a hard white solid. Some varieties are harder than others. (Hydrocal or dental plaster are probably the best types to use for miniatures.) The proportion of plaster to water also helps to determine how hard the plaster will set. It is best to pour water into a polyethylene bowl first and then *sprinkle* the plaster into the water until it forms a small mound above the water. Allow the plaster to slake for two minutes to absorb the water and then stir the mixture with your fingers. Stirring should continue until the plaster begins to thicken, which should be about two to three minutes. If you find lumps, it is because you poured the plaster into the water too fast. Work

244

them out with your fingers. When the mixture is thick enough so that a finger drawn over the surface leaves a slight trace, the plaster is ready to pour.

Making a Rubber Mold

If the positive is porous, coat it by brush with petroleum jelly or a green soap solution, making certain that globs and lumps do not accumulate to obscure details and that the coverage is even. Then at least six layers of rubber (Rubamold) are brushed over the coated surface at thirty-minute intervals. The thickness should reach 1/8 inch to 1/4 inch depending on the size and depth of your positive. After the six applications have dried thoroughly for 24 hours in a warm place, the mold is then peeled away from the positive and ready for a pouring of plaster. After the initial pouring, the rubber mold should be recoated with mineral oil, petroleum jelly, or green soap before casting other plaster parts.

MAKING A RUBBER MOLD FOR PLASTER CASTING

Materials are gathered for making a rubber mold which is excellent for castings of plaster.

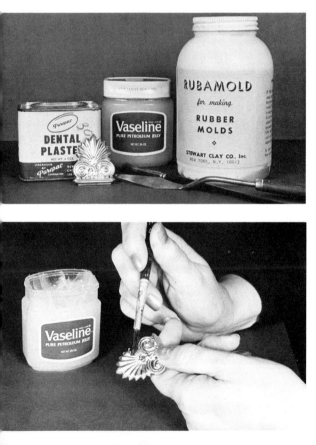

The positive is brushed with a thin layer of petroleum jelly or green soap.

Then six layers of Rubamold are brushed over one half of the coated surface (the front) at 30-minute intervals, until a thickness of 1/8 to 1/4 inch has been reached. (The larger the piece, the thicker the mold should be.)

The piece is removed from the mold revealing an exact replication of the surface.

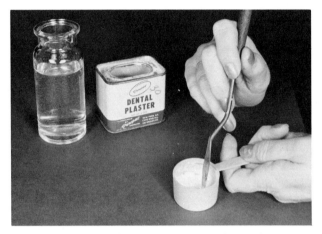

A tablespoon of dental plaster is added to about 1/4 tea-spoon of water at room temperature. The mixture is stirred until it reaches a creamy consistency. If more water is needed, add it drop by drop.

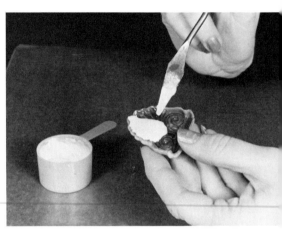

Drop the plaster into the mold with a spatula and pack it into the crevices. (For the first casting, the mold will already be coated; but for subsequent pourings, coat the mold with petroleum jelly or green soap each time.)

This completed casting can be used as an architec-tural or furniture element.

Plaster castings that have been painted with acrylic and then glazed with Krylon or glossy acrylic medium.

WORKING WITH METALS

It is possible to employ all kinds of metalworking techniques when making forms of metal. Copper, brass, silver and gold, lead, pewter, and tin are just some of the metals used in making miniatures.

Silver filigree is one technique used all over the world. Lost wax casting is another ancient popular technique and most applicable for miniature making. Metal turning, repoussé, and metal forging can be employed as well as enameling of metal. Although soldering of metal parts is popular and easy to do, wrought iron work and casting with lead is best left to the specialist. Any technique used to make silver or gold jewelry also is applicable. And perhaps the easiest method is to assemble metal findings, often used for jewelry, carpentry, and leather, into new pieces. Innovation is the key here.

Soldering

Soldering is the process of joining two or more pieces of metal by running molten metal (the solder) between them so that the metal solidifies and the joint is firm. In hard-soldering, the solder has a melting point just slightly lower than that of the metals to be joined, and the metals actually fuse. In soft-soldering, the melting point of the solder is considerably lower and the resulting joint is weaker. When soldering silver, the solder should have the same proportion of silver as the rest of the article. Soft-solder is made of base (nonprecious) metals.

Surfaces to be joined must be made absolutely clean by scraping or filing. The clean metal surfaces are usually coated with flux to encourage the solder to flow as well as to dissolve the oxides that form on metals when they are heated. When these oxides form, metal parts do not join well.

The pieces to be joined are arranged in the proper joining position and, if necessary, are bound together with a temporary binding wire. The piece is then heated with heat from a torch flame or an iron until it is hot enough for the solder to run. After soldering, the piece has to be cleaned, usually by immersion in a pickle solution (a water-diluted nitric or sulphuric acid, usually half and half). If the work is held together with wire, this should be removed before placing the piece in the pickle solution. Further polishing with metal rouges can bring the metal to a high shine.

MAKING A HIGH WHEEL BICYCLE

All the materials are gathered for making a high wheel bicycle (Penny Farthing Bicycle). A jig for the plastic wheel, solder, soldering iron, leather for the seat, and wire.

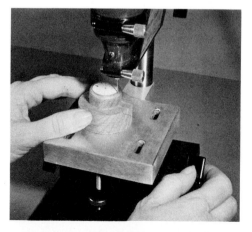

Plastic circles are cut for wheels and holes are drilled in both the large and small wheels using a wooden jig to hold the work while drilling, as well as to provide an indicator as to where the holes are to go.

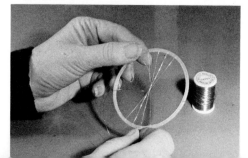

The wheels are then threaded with wire, pulling the wire tautly, to form the spokes.

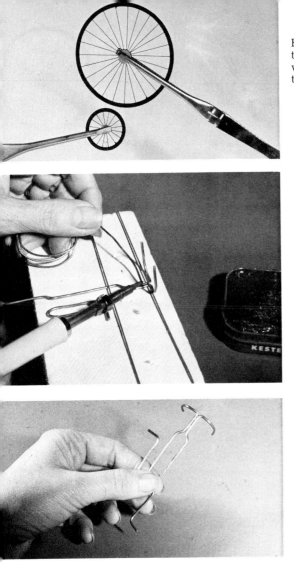

Four wooden circles are sliced from dowels to form the hub of the wheels. Two pieces are used for each wheel, epoxied on either side of the center to form the hub.

Two pieces of wire are bent into handlebars and the front frame including the pedal pieces, one for each side of the bicycle. Then the two parts are soldered together at the fork with 60-40 Resin core solder and Kester's soldering paste.

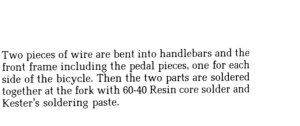

Wire is bent for the shaft that leads from the handlebars to the back wheel. The piece is soldered onto the handlebars, at the top of the fork. The edges of the wire that will attach to the back wheel are flattened so that a tiny (1/8-inch) brass pin will fit in place with pins and epoxy.

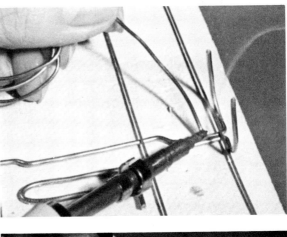

The front fork is glued in place at the wheel hub with two-part epoxy.

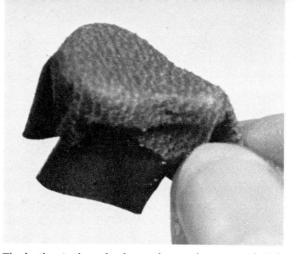

Meanwhile, the seat is carved from 3/8-inch basswood. Skiving leather (a leather lining material) is cut larger than the seat. The leather is moistened, then pressed out over a piece of styrofoam to follow the contours of the seat.

The leather is then glued onto the wooden seat with Velverette, while at the same time stretching and fitting the leather so it fits tightly. Excess is cut off the bottom edge. Gold paper braid that resembles nailheads is glued around the bottom edge of the seat.

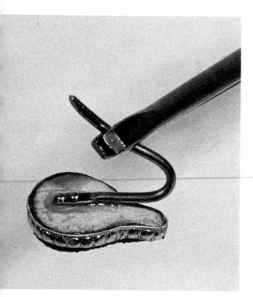

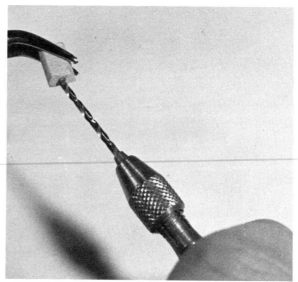

A wire piece is nailed to the seat bottom, using epoxy as well.

Pedals are cut from 1/8-inch basswood, 3/8 inch X 1/4 inch, with a hole hand-drilled in each pedal to accommodate the pedal bar. These attachments are also reinforced with epoxy.

Handlebar ends are cut from 1/8-inch dowel stick to 3/8 inch long. And holes are hand-drilled on the end to fit the wire handlebar. They are glued into place with epoxy. Pedals and handlebar handles, as well as the rest of the metal, are painted with acrylic and glazed with either glossy acrylic medium or Krylon.

A high wheel bicycle.

CHANDELIERS

A Colonial chandelier created by soldering sundry parts together is shown completed and with its various elements.

Parts are soldered together at Weder Enterprises using a gas torch.

Another chandelier—the one at the bottom—duplicates the large wrought iron piece. By Weder Enterprises.

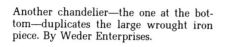

A welded wrought iron candleholder from Weder Enterprises.

A wrought iron piece from Weder Enterprises.

252

Lost Wax Casting

Lost wax casting is an ancient process, known perhaps four thousand years ago. Essentially, the process consists of making a model of the object in wax, encasing the wax model in some fire-resistant material such as plaster, heating this mold so that the wax runs out of vents, and then pouring molten metal in through the same opening so that a perfect replica is formed.

It is possible to purchase lost wax centrifugal casting equipment designed for the hobbyist which contains a centrifugal caster, crucibles, tongs, sometimes burnout ovens for melting out the wax, and torches with which to melt the metal to pouring point. But by far the easiest and perhaps the best way is to form the miniature by modeling it of beeswax or carving it from the polyethylene wax sold by jewelry suppliers for this purpose, and then sending the piece to a firm that specializes in lost wax casting for the jewelry trade.

When the cast piece comes back from the caster, it then needs to be cleaned of any imperfections with dental drills and then polished. This is how most of the miniature tea services, cast brass inkstands, and so on, have been made.

The lost wax process probably is the most efficient way of creating silver accessories, or even brass, for that matter. This sterling silver tea service was made in the lost wax process by Eugene Kupjack.

An assortment of silver in a silver knife box.

An assortment of miniature sterling silver forms by Eugene Kupjack.

Elements of this piece were cast in silver in the lost wax process and then soldered to preforged parts by Eugene Kupjack.

Silver charms as miniature accessories.

Cast silver chess pieces and chessboard by Eugene Kupjack.
The chessboard is done in the marquetry process.

A cast brass inkstand from the Miniature Mart.

METAL WELDING AND CASTING

Welded metal library steps and an umbrella stand made by
the Village Smithy.

Metal is also cast into molds as was this cast
metal Windsor chair by Eugene Kupjack.

Tiffany-style lamp with cast metal base and glass shades.

Cast metal chairs from Germany.

256

Cast metal chairs and table. The chess pieces were cast differently—in the lost wax process. *Courtesy: It's a Small World*

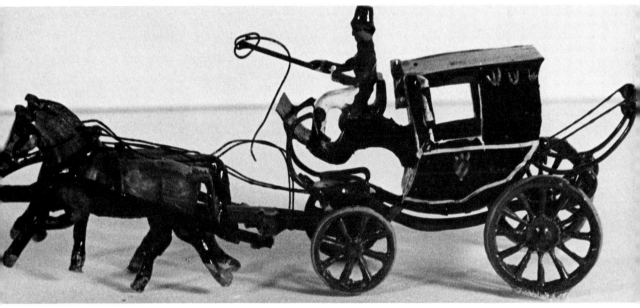

Cast lead carriage from Spain.

Two styles of metal sewing machines from Mexico. *Courtesy: House of Miniatures*

Metal Turning

Metal is turned through use of a jeweler's lathe. This type of lathe is a precision instrument, very much smaller in scale than a wood turning lathe. In the lathe, a metal piece is held horizontally between two adjustable centers, one at each end of the machine, and is rotated with a motor. As the lathe turns, the metal is shaped by applying cutting tools against the rotating metal. Curls of metal are cut away, leaving symmetrical and somewhat geometric shapes. Vases, lamp bases, spittoons, plates, cups, and other such forms can be turned on a lathe. Very often aluminum is used because it is a soft metal.

Turning a brass finial on a jeweler's lathe.

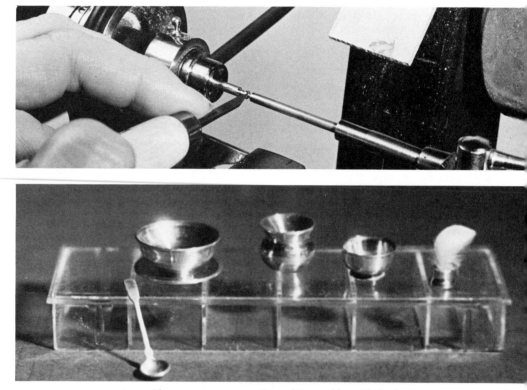

Three pewter parts on the right, possibly made by turning, at Taylor Made Tines. And two pewter pieces on the left made by Paul A. Runyon.

Improvisations with Metal

Jewelry, hardware, and other findings can be assembled in uncommon ways. The only problem, after the composite goes beyond the idea stage, is how to join parts together. Sometimes they can be soldered or wired together, but probably the best way is to apply a spot of a two-part clear epoxy adhesive.

Jewelry parts can be made into chandeliers and lamp bases. Nuts and bolts also can be assembled into fireplace sets, lamp bases, and an assortment of accessories.

Ingenuity and imagination are your most precious "materials."

Three improvised and soldered kitchen utensils. After being joined, the pieces are silver-plated to hide differences in metal colors.

A handforged copper pitcher from Santa Clara de Cobre, Mexico.

Glued and soldered from a demitasse spoon, nuts, bolts and wire, this fireplace set was then silver-plated so that it ended up all one color. It could also have been painted in dull black acrylic to resemble wrought iron.

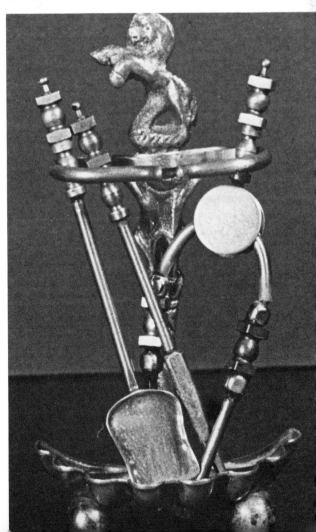

Toleware by Marietta Slayton.

Miniature gas tanks made for model cars and trains are now converted to ...

... cannisters and fire boxes with a bit of cutting, soldering (of holes) and painting.

7 | MAKING MORE ACCESSORIES THROUGH IMPROVISATIONS

Half the fun of miniature making is improvising—coming up with creative and uncommon uses for things and putting them together into something quite different, yet authentic. Next to the satisfaction of making these accessories is the discovery of a source—craftsmen and businesses that have fresh new materials. What it all amounts to is that the miniature environment maker becomes an inveterate collector of anything and everything that has any potential. Eventually these collections of minutiae gain added importance when they are sorted, classified, and stored in special containers complete with labels. This is the storehouse for improvisation, the substance for the laboratory where ideas are transformed from assemblages of anything into what may be a central focus in a room—a crystal chandelier or the clock on a mantel.

Besides collecting seemingly irrelevant parts, the excitement of creating emerges as the bits and pieces are transformed into the miniature semblance of a real thing. When a transparent pill capsule becomes a cover that will protect and enclose a precious tiny sculpture that in turn rests on a base (which also may be nothing more than a wooden nickel); when a nut for a screw becomes a candleholder; when a powder puff is cut into a bathroom rug—whatever—the new form is the "thing of joy" because imagination put it all together. However, along with imagination and creativity, you might also use some wire, nylon fishing line, chain, jewelry findings, epoxy, and patience! These are the main ingredients and requirements that unite what would appear to be disparate elements into a tiny whole.

What follows here is a potpourri of ideas, almost all improvisations. Different uses are found for familiar materials, such as making a fruit compote out of pill capsules, brass eyelets, rivets, brass buttons, epoxy putty, and five-minute epoxy, or creating a Tiffany-type lamp from a Ping-Pong ball. And, sometimes a process is reduced in size just as the item is, such as making a frame and gold-leafing it, or creating an arrangement of beaded flowers.

After you follow some of the adventures in assembling parts to produce miniature accessories, new ideas will occur to you. You will also notice that almost anything can be attached to anything—thank goodness for epoxy!

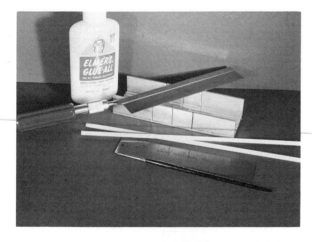

MAKING A GOLD LEAF MINIATURE FRAME

Gather materials for making a gold leaf frame. The miniature miter box and saw are by X-Acto.

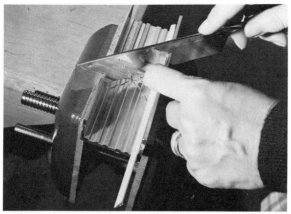

Place miter box in a vise to hold it securely and cut four lengths of molding at 45° angles.

Apply white glue to edges . . .

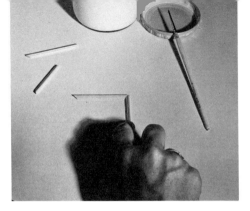

... and place glue-coated sections together over wax paper. Allow twenty minutes for the glue to dry and the frame is ready for gilding. If you have trouble keeping corners together, make a boxlike jig to hold the pieces securely.

While waiting for the glue to dry, gather the gold leafing implements and materials—acrylic modeling paste, sandpaper, gold size, gold leaf, varnish, a brush for the size and varnish, a gilder's brush, and a knife are essential. Bole, a rusty-red acrylic paint, is optional.

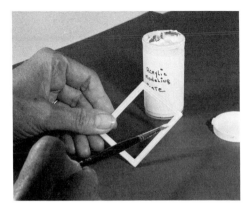

Apply one coat of acrylic modeling paste to create a smooth surface. When dry, wet sand lightly with #400 wet-or-dry sandpaper until smooth.

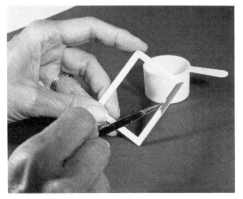

Paint the frame with bole, a rusty-red acrylic paint. This color of undercoat intensifies the gold. Allow to dry for about forty minutes.

Brush on a coating of quick drying gold size.

When the size becomes tacky to touch, in about a half hour (in a dry room), gently slice a piece of gold leaf ...

... rub a bit of petroleum jelly on your wrist and then run the gilder's brush over your wrist. Immediately lift the gold leaf with the brush from the packet and place it on the frame.

Tamp the delicate leaf with a brush in a tamping action. Let the gold leaf dry for 24 hours. Then, with cotton ball, dust away excess leaf.

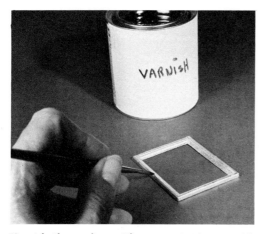 

Varnish the surface with any protective varnish. This is an eggshell varnish that imparts a mat surface.

The basic frame can be changed into a period piece by adding gold findings with epoxy.

Another version of a decorative frame.

In order to make a Federal period mirror, assemble saw,
ruler, varnishes, brushes, sandpaper, epoxy, and decorative
findings.

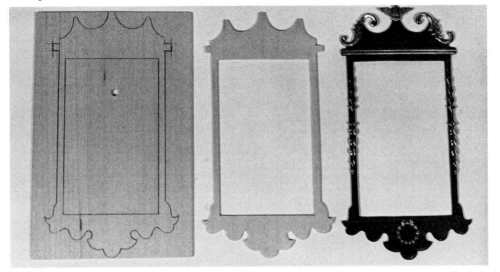

Three main stages in making the frame. On the left,
design is traced on basswood. Areas then are cut away
with a saw. After sanding surfaces and edges smooth,
the wood is stained with wood stain. After the stain
dries, the piece is varnished with two or three coats;
when dry it is sanded, and gold findings are attached
with two-part epoxy. The mirror is glued in place last.

Another version of an ornamented frame.

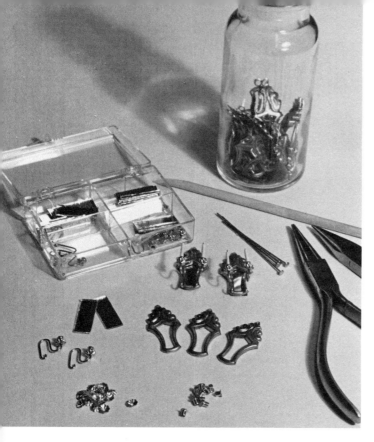

MAKING CANDLE SCONCES

To make a sconce. Brass findings, brass pins, miniature rosettes, a narrow piece of mirror, brass eyelets, and Krazy Glue are gathered.

Attach a rosette to the head of a brass pin with a spot of Krazy Glue.

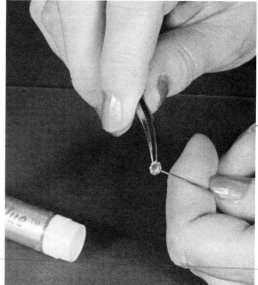

Then glue a brass eyelet to the rosette. This part becomes the candleholder.

With jeweler's pliers, bend the stem of the pin into an S curve around an orange stick or dowel.

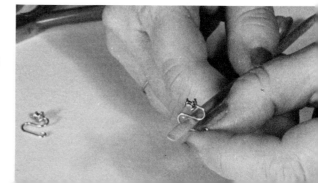

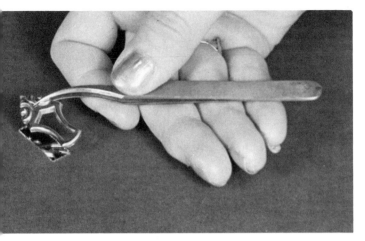

Epoxy a brass finding, which will become a frame, onto the mirror.

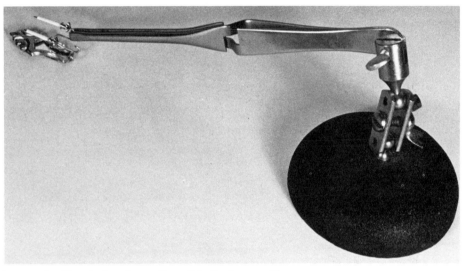

Using a third hand, glue the candle unit to the frame with epoxy. The candles are round toothpicks that have been painted white.

A pair of completed sconces.

MAKING A CLOCK

Assemble materials and tools for making a clock—brass findings, 1/16 inch thick basswood, Liquid Leaf, epoxy, tweezers, and paint brush.

Trace the contours of the clock onto basswood using a template and cut the shape out of the wood with a saw.

Sand with #200 grit sandpaper. Paint the surface with one coat of Liquid Leaf. Allow it to dry.

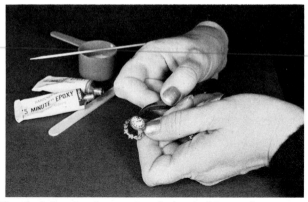

The clock face is a button. Attach the clockface and ornaments with two-part five-minute epoxy.

Add other ornamental trim to the basic shape with epoxy, as well.

The completed clock.

MORE ON CLOCKS

Assemble materials: 1/16 inch basswood with assorted metal findings, five-minute epoxy, India ink, pen, acrylic paint, and brush.

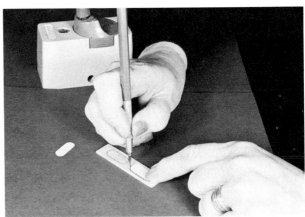

Trace the form from a pattern and cut the two ovals from the basswood. These later will be used as a base for the clock. One is a bit larger than the other.

Glue the two pieces together with white glue.

Paint the wood base with acrylic paint.

Faux-marbling is simulated by painting white lines on the black acrylic surface to imitate marble.

Attach findings with epoxy ...

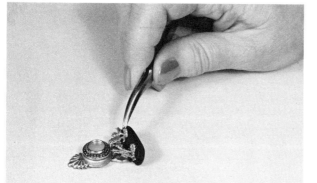

... and glue these to the base.

Draw numerals on the clock with India ink. (A magnifying glass would help here.)

The completed mantel clock.

Variations on the theme.

MAKING BEADED FLOWERS

Assemble materials for making
beaded flowers—tiny beads, fine
brass wire, floral tape, pliers, and
the vase for the flowers.

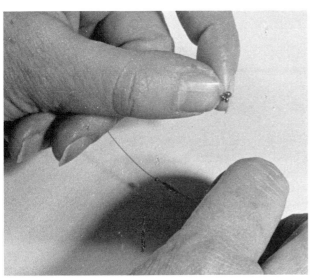

Thread three beads onto a wire and twist the end to make
a petal.

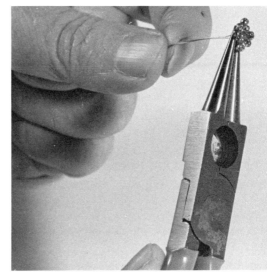

Feed more beads to form a cluster and attach the
"three" bead clusters as leaves. Each time a piece
is added, twist the wire to hold beads securely in
place.

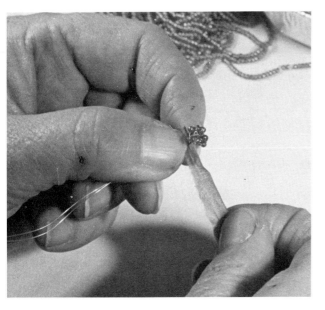

Combine units and wrap the wire
tightly with floral tape. (It is waxy and
sticks to itself.)

Combine, as in this arrangement
made by Grace Andersen.

MAKING A FRUIT COMPOTE

Gather parts: three sizes of brass buttons, top half of empty pill capsules, brass eyelets and rivets, epoxy putty, five-minute epoxy, acrylic paint, and brush.

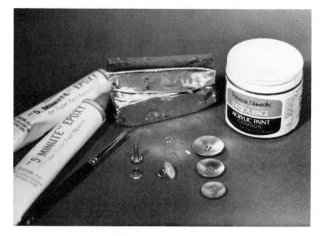

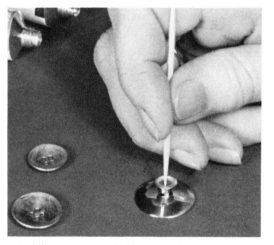

Attach larger section of a brass eyelet to the underside of the largest brass button with five-minute epoxy. This becomes the base or stand.

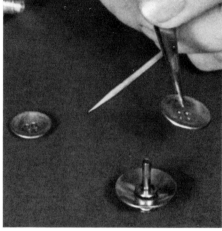

Glue the other longer section of a rivet to the top center of the button and then glue in place the middle-size button. Attach another rivet to that and glue the smallest button to that. There is now a three-tiered compote dish.

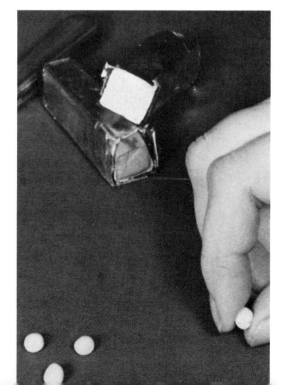

The next procedure involves forming the fruit, in this case apples, for the compote dish. Two-part epoxy putty is metered into equal parts, kneaded until well mixed, and shaped into apple shapes. Stick a toothpick into each apple before the epoxy hardens.

When hard, the "apples" are ready for painting with acrylic paint. The tops of these apples are finished with a blob of white paint to represent a bit of cream.

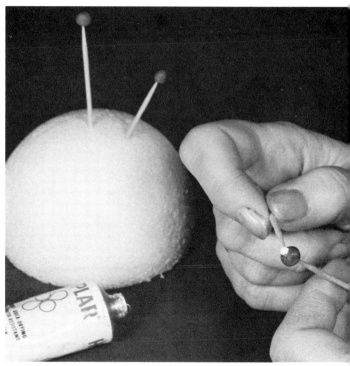

The topmost part of the compote is formed with a glass button and the top of the empty pill capsule which encloses an apple.

The completed compote.

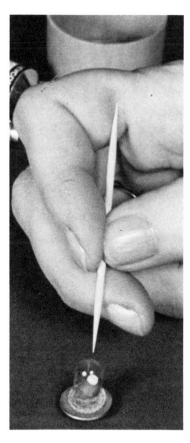

MAKING A "TIFFANY" LAMP

Materials are gathered for making a Tiffany-type lamp. The Ping-Pong ball is the main ingredient.

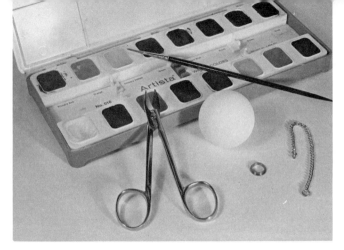

A template is held over the ball to act as a guide and gauge in order to divide the ball into eight segments and to indicate lines for the scallops. The part to be used here is three-quarters of the ball.

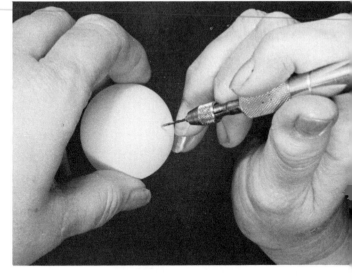

The ball is pierced with a miniature hand drill at the top and bottom.

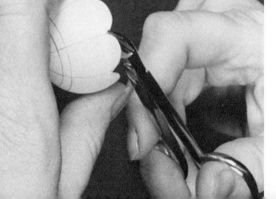

With a cuticle scissors, scallops are cut into the larger section of the ball.

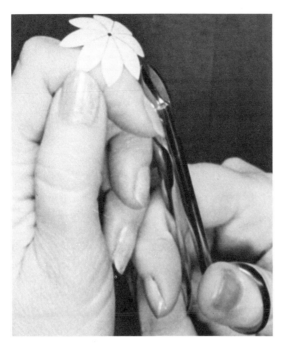

Then points are cut into the smaller part of the ball.

With epoxy, both the top and bottom are attached to a brass (airport) finding that acts as a separator.

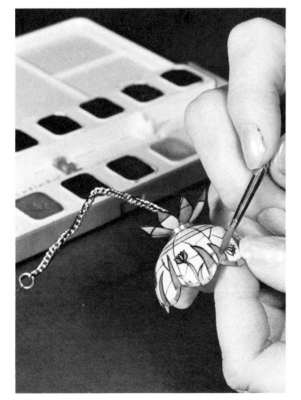

Draw and paint designs with watercolors, colored India ink, or with acrylic paint diluted with water. The color should be intense, yet translucent so that light can penetrate through the color. Black lines simulate lead joints and define color areas. (If you can draw out LePage's Liquid Solder into a thin enough bead, it might be effective here.)

The completed lamp wired and hung with a chain (jewelry finding).

A Victorian chandelier made from assorted findings. *Courtesy: The Peddlers Shop*

Another improvisation, a chandelier. *Collection of Elizabeth Scull*

Brass findings, crystal, and gold beads are assembled into this chandelier by Virginia Merrill.

Beads, crystals, and toothpicks form this candle lamp piece by Virginia Merrill.

An elaborate variation on the theme, an improvisation with beads and findings repeated around a central stem. *Courtesy: The Peddler's Shop*

OTHER IMPROVISATIONS

Lamps from the Peddlers Shop.

Down to earth with materials that work well as floor coverings—stick-on veneer, vinyl and ceramic tiles in mini-mosaics.

An assortment of furniture and compatible accessories by Harry Smith of Barnstable Originals. *Courtesy: Barnstable Originals*

Readable leather-bound book all of 1 inch tall and 2/3 of an inch wide. From the Ginger Jar.

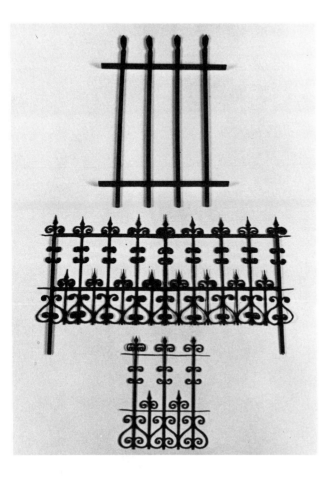

Wrought iron and plastic railings from the Shackman catalog.

Grandma Stover's (Inc.) accessories.

Miniature baskets from Thailand.

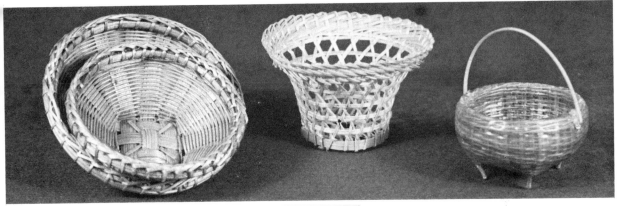

Lacquerware from Thailand. This piece is 7/8 inch tall. The original skeleton for the lacquerware process is a basket which has been coated with many layers of lacquer and then sanded and turned to result in a symmetrical form.

281

MATERIALS AND SOME APPLICATIONS

acrylic findings (spheres, domes, etc.)—accessories, furniture, lamps, bowls, etc.

acrylic gesso—white acrylic heavy coating for ceilings, walls, furniture, accessories, marble finishes, ceramic tile coating

acrylic modeling paste—porcelainlike coatings for kitchen and bathroom furnishings, wall texturing (e.g., stucco, stone, etc.)

acrylic rods—bottles and glasses

acrylic sheeting—furniture, windows, picture frame "glass," accessories

balsa wood—furniture, accessories, trims

basswood—furniture, accessories, trims, mullions, columns, framing, flooring, paneling

beads—chandeliers, flowers

bird gravel—gravel

buckram—floor matting

buttons—dishes, lighting fixtures, etc.

cardboards—various heavy weights—book covers, walls, ceilings, pieced for textures

cellulose acetate sheeting—glass for picture frames or windows

Celotex—rocks, cliffs, architectural surfaces

ceramic—bowls, furniture, appliances, food

coffee stirrers (wood)—floor and wall planking, roof shingles, etc.

cork—simulated brick

crochet—afghans, throw rugs

dried flowers, twigs, grasses—into flower arrangements and plants, e.g., baby's breath, straw flowers, etc.

dried foods—e.g., beans, rice—painted in other-food colors and textures

epoxy putties—accessories, reproduction of food, flowers, furniture embellishments, architectural details, etc.

etcetera—this is a big one—made up of everything we did not think of!

fabrics—assorted wall, window, furniture, floor coverings, pillows, bedspreads, wall hangings, single pattern framed as picture, lampshades, accessories such as tablecloths, napkins, linens in closet, etc.

fiberglass and polyester resin—forming of contemporary furniture, construction of unusual architectural shapes such as domes

flocking (soft, woolly, velvetlike fiber) coverings for floors, walls, furniture

foams, expanded rigid (styrene and urethane)—furniture, walls, ceilings, roofs, siding, sidewalks

foams, flexible—chair padding, pillows

fusible pellets—crystallike plastic beads, fused into bowls, panels, parts for lamps, etc.

gelatin pill casings—lamps and lighting fixtures, glasses and cups, apothecary jars

handkerchiefs (lace trim)—curtains, bed-curtains, etc.

knitting—throw rugs

lace—covered with LePage's liquid solder or with black polyester resin as wrought iron ornamentation

linoleum (for carving) flooring, carved into textures, e.g., tiles

loofa sponge—garden textures

map tacks—drawer pulls

masonite—floors, walls, ceilings

metal findings—chandeliers, lamps, fireplace accessories, clocks, sconces, architectural and furniture details, etc.

metal foils—representing metal surfaces such as corrugated metal (over corrugated cardboard), tinsel paintings

metal sheeting—complex building forms

metal wire, chain, rods, dowels, and tubing—various accessories such as lighting fixtures, furniture, fencing, railing, etc.

metallized Mylar and/or diffracting grating—simulated mother-of-pearl

nylon stockings (strips)—braided rugs

papers, decorative and otherwise—wall coverings, cabinet and drawer lining, book papers, embossed paper for shingles, brick, mosaic, etc.

patterned silk scarves—rugs, curtains, etc.

petit point—upholstery textile, rugs

Ping-Pong balls—globes, lamps and shades, furniture parts

pinheads (various kinds)—drawer pulls and simulated nailheads plaster—accessories such as sconces, architectural details, sculptures, reproduction of foods, molds, etc.

plastic boxes (small)—base for veneer covering for furniture, cabinets, etc.

plasticene—sculptures, texturing of architectural surfaces, plant parts, earth

plywood—wall members, ceiling, roofs

polyester resins—casting of any object from furniture to accessories and pouring of stained glass windows, cast to resemble water for fountains, pools, etc.

polyethylene doilies (coated with metallic Rub 'n Buff)—wrought iron patterns

polyethylene scrap—melted down into plant parts

powder puffs—bathroom mats

prints of scenes—distant backgrounds

ribbons (various widths)—fine weaves—wall covering, upholstery, drapery, etc.

sands (various textures)—with glue—sidewalks, flooring, walls (stone), can be combined with plasticene or polyester resin

sawdust—ground cover, floral elements

Sculpt Metal Art Brite—metal surface coverings, sculptures, metal ac-

sealing wax (various colors)—modeling and carving fruits, flowers

silicone—plant parts, molds

skiving leather—thin leather for upholstery, bookbindings

solder, liquid—stained glass partitions, small accessories, e.g., spoons, etc.

sponges (various textures)—landscaping elements—shrubs, trees

tapes, decorative—trims and textured effects for furniture, walls, etc.

tatting (fine thread)—bedspreads, doilies

thread spools (various sizes, empty)—plant stands and planters, umbrella stands, table bases, stools, lamp bases, wheels, toys, etc.

tinfoil—mirrors

toothpicks, applicator sticks—parts of anything, "bamboo" trellis

wax—surface texturing, e.g., bricks, shingles, reproduction of foods such as ice cream desserts, sculptures, the original of anything to be cast in metals—lost wax process

wood, e.g., obechi, pine, beech, linden, sycamore, spruce, mahogany, etc.—furniture and almost all architectural details

wood veneers—furniture, walls, floors, ceiling beams, and architectural wood details

wool—animal skin rugs, upholstery, carpeting

write-on gold foils (used in greeting cards)—markings on ceramics and leather bookbindings

yarns and threads—assorted wall, window, furniture, and floor coverings

BIBLIOGRAPHY

DOLLHOUSES AND MINIATURES

Benson, A. C., and Weaver, Sir Lawrence, ed. *The Book of the Queen's Doll's House.* London: Methuen & Co., Ltd., 1924, 2 volumes.

Dorsett, Helen. *A Cabinetmaker's Guide for Doll House Furniture.* Vol. 1, 1964, Vol. 2, 1969. Available through Doll Books, 4701 Queensburg Rd., Riverdale, Md. 20840.

Hohauser, Sanford. *Architectural and Interior Models, Design and Construction.* New York: Van Nostrand Reinhold, 1970.

Hughes, Bernard and Therle. *Small Antique Furniture.* New York–Washington: Frederick A. Praeger.

Jacobs, Flora Gill. *Dolls' Houses in America.* New York: Charles Scribner's Sons, 1974.

_____. *A History of Doll Houses.* New York: Charles Scribner's Sons, 1953.

_____. *A World of Doll Houses.* New York: Rand McNally & Co., 1965.

_____, and Faurholt, Estrid. *A Book of Dolls and Doll Houses.* Vermont and Japan: Charles E. Tuttle Co., 1967.

Johnson, Audrey. *How to Make Dolls' Houses.* London: Wm. Clowes & Sons Ltd., 1957.

———. *Furnishing Dolls' Houses.* Newton Centre, Mass.: Charles Branford Co., 1972.

Latham, Jean. *Collecting Miniature Antiques.* New York: Charles Scribner's Sons, 1972.

———. *Dolls' Houses, A Personal Choice.* New York: Charles Scribner's Sons, 1969.

McClinton, Katharine Morrison. *The Complete Book of Small Antique Collecting.* New York: Bramhall, 1965.

Moore, Colleen. *Colleen Moore's Doll House.* Garden City, N.Y.: Doubleday & Co., Inc., 1974.

Musgrave, Clifford. *Queen Mary's Dolls' House and Dolls Belonging to H.M. the Queen.* London: Garrod & Lofthouse International, Ltd., 1970.

O'Brien, Marian Maeze. *The Collectors Guide to Doll Houses and Doll House Miniatures.* New York: Hawthorne Books, Inc., 1974.

Schiffer, Herbert F. and Peter B. *Miniature Antique Furniture.* Pennsylvania: Livingston Publishing Co., 1972.

Thorne, Mrs. Warde. *American Rooms in Miniature.* Chicago: The Art Institute of Chicago, 1962.

———. *European Rooms in Miniature.* Chicago: The Art Institute of Chicago, 1962.

Williams, Guy R. *Making a Miniature House.* Oxford: Oxford University Press, 1964.

Worrell, Estelle Ansley. *Americana in Miniature.* New York: Van Nostrand Reinhold Company, 1973.

FURNITURE

Aronson, Joseph. *The Encyclopedia of Furniture.* New York: Crown Publishers, Inc., 1965.

Feirer, John L. *Cabinetmaking and Millwork.* Peoria, Del.: Chas. A. Bennett Co., Inc., 1970.

Hayward, Charles H. *Practical Veneering.* London: Evans Bros., 1971.

Hinckley, F. Lewis. *A Directory of Antique Furniture.* New York: Bonanza Books, 1953.

Joyce, Ernest. *The Encyclopedia of Furniture Making.* New York: Drake Publishers, Inc., 1973.

Margon, Lester. *Masterpieces of American Furniture.* New York: Architectural Book Publishing Co., 1965.

———. *Masterpieces of European Furniture.* New York: Architectural Book Publishing Co., 1968.

Molesworth, H. D., and Kenworthy-Browne, John. *Three Centuries of Furniture in Color.* New York: The Viking Press, 1972.

O'Neil, Isabel. *The Art of the Painted Finish for Furniture and Decoration.* New York: William Morrow & Co., Inc., 1971.

Sack, Albert. *Fine Points of Furniture: Early American.* New York: Crown Publishers, Inc., 1950.

Strange, Thomas A. *English Furniture Decoration Woodwork and Allied Arts.* New York: Bonanza Books.

GENERAL

Griswold, Lester and Kathleen. *The New Handicraft.* New York: Van Nostrand Reinhold Company, 1972.

Moseley, Spencer; Johnson, Pauline; and Koenig, Hazel. *Crafts Design.* Belmont, Calif.: Wadsworth Publishing Co., Inc., 1963.

Zechlin, Ruth. *Complete Book of Handicrafts.* Newton Centre, Mass.: Charles T. Branford Co., 1967.

GLASSBLOWING

Wheeler, E. L. *Scientific Glassblowing.* New York: Interscience Publishers, Inc., 1958.

MISCELLANEOUS

Child, Peter. *The Craftsman Woodturner.* London: G. Bell & Sons, 1973.

Fraser, Antonio. *A History of Toys.* London: Delacorte Press, 1966.

Joy, Edward T. *The Country Life Book of Clocks.* Great Britain: Country Life Books, The Hamlyn Publishing Group Ltd., 1967.

Kenny, John B. *The Complete Book of Pottery Making.* Radnor, Pa.: Chilton Books, 1963.

Lewis, A. W. *Basic Bookbinding.* New York: Dover Publications, Inc., 1957.

Newman, Thelma R. *Contemporary Decoupage.* New York: Crown Publishers, Inc., 1972.

———. *Leather as Art and Craft.* New York: Crown Publishers, Inc., 1973.

———, Jay H., and Lee S. *Paper as Art and Craft.* New York: Crown Publishers, Inc., 1973.

PLASTICS

Newman, Jay H. and Lee S. *Plastics for the Craftsman.* New York: Crown Publishers, Inc., 1972.

Newman, Thelma R. *Plastics as Art Form.* Radnor, Pa.: Chilton Books, 1964.

TEXTILE ARTS

Birrell, Verla. *The Textile Arts.* New York: Harper & Row, 1972.

Hollander, Annette. *Decorative Papers and Fabrics.* New York: Van Nostrand Reinhold Company, 1971.

Newman, Thelma R. *Quilting, Patchwork, Appliqué, and Trapunto.* New York: Crown Publishers, Inc., 1974.

Rome, Carol Cheney. *A New Look at Bargello.* New York: Crown Publishers, Inc., 1973.

_____, and Devlin, Georgia French. *A New Look at Needlepoint.* New York: Crown Publishers, Inc., 1972.

Wilson, Jean. *Weaving Is for Anyone.* New York: Reinhold Publishing Corp., 1967.

Znamierowski, Nell. *Step-by-Step Weaving.* Racine, Wisc.: Golden Press, 1967.

BOOKS ON MINIATURES

Paul Ruddell
4701 N. Queensbury Road
Riverdale, Maryland 20840
  *Specializes in books on
  miniatures*

PUBLICATIONS

The Berry Hill News
Canyon Route
Gallatin Gateway, Montana 59730
  *A newsletter for children about
  dollhouses and miniatures ages
  7–14*

Carsten's Publications
PO Box 700
Newton, New Jersey 07860
  Railroad Modelcraftsmen

Doll House and Miniature News
#3 Orchard Lane
Kirkwood, Missouri 63122
  Marian O'Brien, Editor

Doll Reader
4701 N. Queensbury Road
Riverdale, Maryland 20840
  Lists publications 4 times a year

International Doll House News
56 Lincoln Wood
Haywards Heath, RH 16, 1LH
Sussex, England

Lightner Publishing Co.
1006 South Michigan Avenue
Chicago, Illinois 60605
  Hobbies—a trade paper

Miniature Gazette
Box 2621
Brookhurst Center
Anaheim, California 92804

Motts Miniature Workshop News
PO Box 5514
Sunny Station Hills
Fullerton, California 92633

Nutshell News
1035 Newkirk Drive
La Jolla, California 92037
  Catherine B. MacLaren, Editor

Yankee Magazine
Yankee, Inc.
Dublin, New Hampshire 03444

SUPPLY SOURCES

ACCESSORIES

Barnstable Originals
Harry W. Smith
50 Harden Avenue
Camden, Maine 04843

Bassett Antiques
7102 Stauton Avenue
Buena Park, California 90620

Bespoke Miniatures by Paul
  McNeely
R.R. #2 Box 453
Liberty, Missouri 64068
  Tricycles
  Bicycles
  High Wheeler
  Wheels

Broadswords Miniatures
68 Blackburn Road
Summit, New Jersey 07901
  Colonial accessories
  Nautical accessories
  Hand-painted furniture

C & C Imports
Arts & Crafts Supplies
North East Seventh Street
Grand Prairie
Dallas County, Texas
  Miniature baskets
  Flowers, plants
  Kitchen and country store
    accessories

Cathy's Miniatures
22 Surrey Run
Williamsville, New York 14221
  Food items
  Treenware
  Gazebo

Chestnut Hill Studio
Box 38
Churchville, New York 14428

Craft Patterns
A. Neely Hall Productions
Elmhurst, Illinois 60126

Thomas Deveraux
Hollywood Tower, Apt. 27J
5701 N. Sheridan
Chicago, Illinois 60660

The Doll House Factory
Box 456
157 Main Street
Lebanon, New Jersey 08833
Cedar shakes

The Dollhouse Factory
PO Box 2232
Sunnyvale, California 94087

Doreydorf Dollhouses
97 Gorham Road
Fairfield, Connecticut 06430

The Enchanted Doll House
Manchester Center
Manchester, Vermont 05255

Enchanted Toy Shop
23812 Lorain Road
North Olmsted, Ohio 44070

The Ginger Jar
6133 Wakefield Drive
Sylvania, Ohio 43560
Candles
Lanterns
Curtain rods
Shutters

House of Miniatures
PO Box 1816
Santa Fe, New Mexico 87501

It's a Small World
542 Lincoln Avenue
Winnetka, Illinois 60093

Joen Ellen Kanze
26 Palmer Avenue
N. White Plains, New York 10603

Jean Knoop
Blackburn Road
Summit, New Jersey 07901

Mini Mundus
1030 Lexington Avenue
New York, New York 10021

Mini Things by Suzanne
5600 East Oxford Avenue
Englewood, Colorado 80110
Chandeliers

The Miniature Mart & Peddlers Shop
Dept. NN
883 39th Avenue
San Francisco, California 94121
Chandeliers
Dinnerware

Miniatures by Marty
388 Wildwood Drive
Holland, Michigan 49423
Lamps, etc.

The Mouse Hole
111 Eagle Rock Avenue
Roseland, New Jersey 07068

Pickwick Miniatures
PO Box 297
Glenview, Illinois 60025
Food items
Household items
Lamps

Betty Seidel Shops
Cherryville Inn
Cherryville, Pennsylvania 18035

South Shore Woman's Exchange
60 South Street
Hingham, Massachusetts 02043
Chandeliers

Paige Thornton
316 Clairmont Road, NE
Atlanta, Georgia 30329

Wee-un's
40 Laurel Street
E. Weymouth, Massachusetts
02189

Margaret Whitton
RFD #1 Hut Hill Road
Bridgewater, Connecticut 06752

ADHESIVES

Barge Cement Division
National Starch & Chemical Corp.
100 Jacksonville Road
Towaco, New Jersey 07082

Borden Chemical Company
350 Madison Avenue
New York, New York 10017
Elmer's Glue

Columbia Cement Co.
159 Hanse
Freeport, New York 11520
*Quik Stik® rubber cement for
urethane foam*

Craftsman All-Purpose Cement
At all Tandy Leather Company
stores

Devcon Corporation
Endicott Street
Danvers, Massachusetts 01923
Epoxy

Fasson Products
250 Chester Street
Painesville, Ohio 44077
*Clear cold mounting double-faced
tape #333*

ICI America, Inc.
151 South Street
Stamford, Connecticut 06901
*A two-part acrylic
monomer/polymer cured with
a peroxide catalyst. A good
adhesive for acrylic and for
making small castings.
Tensol Cement 7*

Slomon's Labs, Inc.
32-45 Hunter's Point Avenue
Long Island City, New York 11101
Sobo, Quik, Velverette

3M Company
135 W. 50th Street
New York, New York 10020
*3M adhesive for polystyrene foam
or polyurethane foam
EC-2296*

Tra-Con, Inc.
55 North Street
Medford, Massachusetts 02155
*Clear, water-white epoxy
adhesive in a Bipax container
Tra-Con Bipax*

U.S. Plywood Corp.
2305 Superior Street
Kalamazoo, Michigan 49003
Weldwood Contact Cement

BUTTONS

J H B Imports, Inc.
2131 South Jasmine
Denver, Colorado 80222

CASTING

Abbey Materials Corp.
116 W. 29th Street
New York, New York 10001

CERAMICS

Chestnut Hill Studio
Box 38
Churchville, New York 14428

The Ginger Jar
6133 Wakefield Drive
Sylvania, Ohio 43560

Jemil Exclusives Studio
South Main at Devil's Lane
Walworth, Wisconsin 53184
*Bakery goods
Porcelain items*

Jean Knoop
Blackburn Road
Summit, New Jersey 07901

Frieda Leininger
3620 SW 17th Street
Miami, Florida 33145

Deborah McKnight
Featherly Road
Morristown, New Jersey 07960

Mini Things by Suzanne
5600 East Oxford Avenue
Englewood, Colorado 80110

Jean Townsend
415 Manzano NE
Albuquerque, New Mexico 87108
*Porcelain
Items for country kitchen, general
store
Southwest items*

CLAY

Stewart Clay Co., Inc.
133 Mulberry Street
New York, New York 10013
*Rubamold for making rubber
molds*

COLOR

Alcan Metal Powders
PO Box 290
Elizabeth, New Jersey 07207
  Metal powders in aluminum,
    bronze, copper, lead, etc.

Schwartz Chemical Co., Inc.
50-01 Second Street
Long Island City, New York 11101
  Transparent lacquers and dip
    dyes for acrylics
  Rez-N-Lac MM®

COMPLETE-LINE
PLASTICS SUPPLIERS

Abbeon Cal, Inc.
123-21AB Gray Avenue
Santa Barbara, California 93101
  Complete line of plastics and
    equipment

Ain Plastics
65 Fourth Avenue
New York, New York 10003
  A wide range of sheets, resins,
    and plastic findings

Almac Plastics of New York, Inc.
721 East Lincoln Avenue
PO Box 1121
Rahway, New Jersey 07065

American Acrylic Corp.
173 Marine Street
Farmingdale, New York 11735

Cadillac Plastics and Chemical Co.
15841 Secons Avenue
PO Box 810
Detroit, Michigan 48232
  Polyester resin, Plexiglas acrylic,
    and an assortment of many
    other plastic products, available
    throughout North America

Industrial Plastics
324 Canal Street
New York, New York 10013
  A jobber of a complete range of
    plastic resins and findings as
    well as blow-molded acrylic
    domes in various dimensions

The Plastics Factory
119 Avenue D
New York, New York 10009

Saks Arts and Crafts
207 N. Milwaukee Street
Milwaukee, Wisconsin 53202

Alec Tiranti, Ltd.
70 High Street
Theale, Berkshire, England
  Complete line of plastics and
    equipment

Trylon Ltd.
Wollaston Northants NN97Q
England
  Complete line of plastics and
    equipment

CORK

Bradley Enterprises
Main Street
Bradley Beach, New Jersey 07720

Dodge Cork Co.
Lancaster, Pennsylvania 17604

DOLLHOUSES

Bassett Antiques
7102 Stauton Avenue
Buena Park, California 90620

Cathy's Miniatures
22 Surrey Run
Williamsville, New York 14221
  Shops

Gretchen Deans
11 Meadow Lane
New Canaan, Connecticut 06840

The Doll House
3798 Roswell Road, NE
Atlanta, Georgia 30305
  Custom-made

The Doll House Factory
Box 456
157 Main Street
Lebanon, New Jersey 08833

Doreydorf Dollhouses
97 Gorham Road
Fairfield, Connecticut 06430
  Houses and kits

The Enchanted Doll House
Manchester Center Dept. NN064
Vermont 05255

Joen Ellen Kanze
26 Palmer Avenue
N. White Plains, New York 10603

The Lilliput Shop
5955 SW 179th Avenue
Beaverton, Oregon 97005

Bill Muller—Wooden Toys
Rock Hill Industrial Park
87 Commerce Drive
Telford, Pennsylvania 18969

Eleanor Scholz
410 Main Street
Boonton, New Jersey 07005
  Victorian

Winbon Creations
3900 Paradise Drive
Tiburon, California 94920

DOLLS

The Lilliput Shop
5955 SW 179th Avenue
Beaverton, Oregon 97005

Microbius
534 Red Haw Road
Dayton, Ohio 45405

Minutiques
82b Trafalgar Street
Brighton BN 1 4 EB Sussex
England
  Poured wax dolls

Irma Park
7541 Ninth Street
Buena Park, California 90620

DYES FOR COLORING

Fezan Colors
Fezandie & Sperrie, Inc.
103 Lafayette Street
New York, New York 10013

Fibrec
2795 16th Street
San Francisco, California 94103

Hazel Pearson
4128 Temple City Boulevard
Rosemead, California 91770

Rit Dyes
Best Food Company
Indianapolis, Indiana 46206

FABRICS

Lillian A. Gaines
212 S 6th Street
Independence, Kansas 67301
  Handwoven coverlets

Jean Mason ·
45 Nelson Street
Quincy, Massachusetts 02169
  Handmade quilts

Stacy Fabrics Corp.
469 Seventh Avenue
New York, New York 10018
  Fusible webbing

Willoughby's Eighteenth Century
PO Box 918
Los Altos, California 94022

FINDINGS

Bergen Arts & Crafts
PO Box 689
Salem, Massachusetts
  Brass findings
  Catalog available

Boutique Trims
PO Drawer P
21200 Pontiac Trail
South Lyon, Michigan 48178
  Brass findings, etc.

Eastern Findings
19 West 34th Street
New York, New York 10001
  Brass findings

FINDINGS—PLASTIC

Ace Plastic Company
91-30 Van Wyck Expressway
Jamaica, New York 11435
   Acrylic balls, rods, and tubes

Hastings Plastics, Inc.
1704 Colorado Avenue
Santa Monica, California 90404
   *Full gamut of plastic supplies
   from release agents to Mylar
   film to resins*

FLOWERS

Arlene's Memories in Miniature
5521 East Morris
Wichita, Kansas 67218
   Pure silk flowers

Pickwick Miniatures
PO Box 297
Glenview, Illinois 60025
   Flower arrangements

Posy Patch
Box 38123
Atlanta, Georgia 30334

FURNITURE

Hernania Anslinger
320 South Ralph Street
Spokane, Washington 99202

April Day Creations
1210 W. Custer Place
Denver, Colorado 80223
   Plastic contemporary

Arlene's Memories in Miniature
5521 East Morris
Wichita, Kansas 67218

Barnstable Originals
Harry W. Smith
50 Harden Avenue
Camden, Maine 04843

Bassett Antiques
7102 Stanton Avenue
Buena Park, California 90620

Blue Swan Studio
Lee's Hill Road
New Vernon, New Jersey 07976
   *Chinoiserie and other
   custom-made furniture*

Carlson's Custom Crafts
671 Bender Lane
West Chicago, Illinois 60185

Cathy's Miniatures
22 Surrey Run
Williamsville, New York 14221

Chestnut Hill Studio
Box 38
Churchville, New York 14428

D & E Miniatures
PO Box 2117
Culver City, California 90230

The Doll House
3798 Roswell Road, NE
Atlanta, Georgia 30305

The Doll House Factory
PO Box 2232
Sunnyvale, California 94087

The Doll House Factory
Box 456
157 Main Street
Lebanon, New Jersey 08833

Dolphin Originals
Robert Bernhard
7302 Hasbrook Avenue
Philadelphia, Pennsylvania 19111
   Wicker and upholstered

The Enchanted Doll House
Manchester Center
Dept NN064
Vermont 05255

Enchanted Toy Shop
23812 Lorain Road
North Olmsted, Ohio 44070

John Flint
600 Davis Street
Evanston, Illinois 60201

The Ginger Jar
6133 Wakefield Drive
Sylvania, Ohio 43560

A. and S. Grainger
613 Oxford House Emanuel
Ann Arbor, Michigan 48104

House of Miniatures
PO Box 1816
Santa Fe, New Mexico 87501

It's a Small World
542 Lincoln Avenue
Winnetka, Illinois 60093

Jocko Johnson
263652 Via California
Capistrano Beach, California 92624
   Hand-carved modern

Joen Ellen Kanze
26 Palmer Avenue
N. White Plains, New York

The Miniature Mart & Ped-
   dlers Shop
Dept. NN
883 39th Avenue
San Francisco, California 94121
   Victorian furniture

Miniatures by Garilyn
74 Georgina Street
Chula Vista, California 92010
   Handcrafted oak

Miniatures Ltd.
161 Linden Drive
Fair Haven, New Jersey 07701

Minutiques
82b Trafalgar Street
Brighton BN 1
4 EB Sussex, England

Morley Studio
16752 Cooper Lane
Huntington Beach, California 92647

The Mouse Hole
111 Eagle Rock Avenue
Roseland, New Jersey 07068

Mrs. Mell Prescott
Box 177
Warrenville, Connecticut 06278
   Victorian
   Chippendale
   Queen Anne

South Shore Woman's Exchange
60 South Street
Hingham, Massachusetts 02043

Paige Thornton
316 Clairmont Road, NE
Atlanta, Georgia 30329

Betty Valentine
114 E. New State Road
Manchester, Connecticut 06040

Wee "C" Shop
104 W. Vallette
Elmhurst, Illinois 60126

M. White
4290 NW 10th Street
Pompano Beach, Florida 33063

Pamela White Miniatures
12 Rutland Square
Boston, Massachusetts 02118

Margaret Whitton
RFD #1 Hut Hill Road
Bridgewater, Connecticut 06752

Willoughby's Eighteenth Century
PO Box 918
Los Altos, California 94022

Philip Wilson Handcrafted
   Miniatures
Terrapin Ridge
Elizabeth, Illinois 61028

Woodworks by John R. Adams
Junction Road
Brookfield Center, Connecticut 06805

Woody's Hand Crafted Miniatures
PO Box 3211
Green Bay, Wisconsin 54303

GLASS

Milton Breeden
111 North 5th Street
Millville, New Jersey 08332

The Doll House Factory
Box 456
157 Main Street
Lebanon, New Jersey 08833
   Stained glass

David Dorsi
240 Morris Street
Stirling, New Jersey 07980

Glass Blowers Workshop
1212 South Coast Highway
Laguna Beach, California 92651

The Lilliput Shop
5955 SW 179th Avenue
Beaverton, Oregon 97005

Miniature Artistic Glass Blowing
198 Pelham Street
Pembroke, Massachusetts 02359

Minutiques
82b Trafalgar Street
Brighton BN 1 4 EB Sussex
England

Something Different Miniatures
PO Box 1628
FDR Station
New York, New York 10022
   Cut glass perfume bottles
   Mirrors

Yankee Heirlooms
9942 Continental Drive
Huntington Beach, California
 92646
(Kaye H. MacLeod)

GLASS SUPPLIERS

Fisher Scientific Company
Central Offices
711 Forbes Avenue
Pittsburgh, Pennsylvania 15219

Scientific Glass SGA
735 Broad Street
Bloomfield, New Jersey 07003

LEATHER

A. C. Products
422 Hudson Street
New York, New York 10001

Berman Leather
147 South Street
Boston, Massachusetts 02111

Caldwell Lace Leather Co.
Auburn, Kentucky 42206

J. P. Fliegel Co.
PO Box 505
Gloversville, New York 12078

Charles Horowitz & Sons, Inc.
25 Great Jones Street
New York, New York 10014

Saks Arts and Crafts
207 N. Milwaukee Street
Milwaukee, Wisconsin 53202

M. Siegel Co., Inc.
114 South Street
Boston, Massachusetts 02111

Talas
Division of Technical Library Ser-
 vice
104 Fifth Avenue
New York, New York 10011
 Skiver leather

Tandy Leather Company stores

LIGHTING

Illinois Hobbycraft
12 S. Fifth Street
Geneva, Illinois 60134
 *Bulbs, fixtures, and apparatus
 Tools*

MACHINES AND TOOLS

All-Purpose Machines

Dremel Manufacturing Division
4915 21st Street
Racine, Wisconsin 53406
 *Dremel Moto-Shop complete with
 saw, flexible shaft drill, buffing
 and sanding, wood turning
 lathe
 Dremel Moto-Tool for drilling,
 routing, and engraving
 Variable speed controls—foot
 pedal
 Accessories*

Unimat
American Edelstaal, Inc.
1 Atwood Avenue
Tenafly, New Jersey 07670
 *Multipurpose
 Machine tool*

Cutters

Abbeon Cal, Inc.
123-21AB Gray Avenue
Santa Barbara, California 93101
 *Excellent hot wire cutters
 Models PK 14, PK 2414, 9050*

Science Related Materials
Box 1422
Jonesville, Wisconsin 53545
 Hot-wire cutter for rigid foams

Drill Bits

AAA Saw and Tool Service & Supply Co.
1401-07 Washington Boulevard
Chicago, Illinois 60607
 Router bits & wheel brushes

Henry L. Hanson Co.
25 Union Street
Worcester, Massachusetts 01608
 *High-speed drills for acrylic,
 developed by Rohm and Haas
 Co.*

Knives

C. S. Osborne Tool Company
125 Jersey Street
Harrison, New Jersey 07029

X-Acto Precision Tools, Inc.
48-41 Van Dam Street
Long Island City, New York 11101

Tools

All Craft Tool & Supply Co.
215 Park Avenue
Hicksville, New York 11801

Anchor Tool & Supply Co.
12 John Street
New York, New York 10038

Bergen Arts & Crafts
PO Box 689
Salem, Massachusetts 01970
Small tools, files, saws, etc.
Catalog available

Dick Blick
PO Box 1267
Galesburg, Illinois 61401

Brookstone Company
13 Brookstone Building
Peterborough, New Hampshire
03458
Hard-to-find tools
Catalog available

CCM:Arts & Crafts, Inc.
9520 Baltimore Avenue
College Park, Maryland 20740

Colbert Industries
10107 Adella Avenue
South Gate, California 90280
Panavise

Conover & Quayle, Inc.
17 West 47th Street
New York, New York 10036
Tweezers, files, vises, soldering
tools, lathes, gauges, drills,
casting materials

Economy Handicrafts, Inc.
47-11 Francis Lewis Boulevard
Flushing, New York 11361

Force Machinery Company
2271 Route 22
Union, New Jersey 07083
Power tools (Dremel, Unimat)
Hand tools
Accessories

C. S. Osborne Tool Company
125 Jersey Street
Harrison, New Jersey 07029

Saks Arts & Crafts
207 N. Milwaukee Street
Milwaukee, Wisconsin 53202

Ungar
Division of Eldon Industries, Inc.
Compton, California 90220
Soldering iron

Woodcraft Supply Corp.
313 Montvale Avenue
Woburn, Massachusetts 01801
Turning tools, saws, vises, clamps,
files
Catalog available

METAL

Art-Brite Chemical Corp.
81 Broadway
Jersey City, New Jersey 07306
Art-Brite
Model-Metal
Modeling aluminum compound

Bergen Arts & Crafts
PO Box 689
Salem, Massachusetts 01970
Brass findings
Catalog

Brookstone
13 Brookstone Building
Peterborough, New Hampshire
03458
Brass tubing
Solid rods
Catalog

Colonial Craftsmen
PO Box 337
Cape May, New Jersey 08204
Pewter accessories

Copper Corner
300 E. Devonia Avenue
Mt. Vernon, New York 10552
Copper accessories

Crafts Manufacturing Co.
72 Massachusetts Avenue
Lunenburg, Massachusetts 01462
Unpainted miniature trays

Golden Ball Shop
Colonial Williamsburg
Williamsburg, Virginia 23185
Silver miniature charms

Eugene Kupjack
1200 South Fairview Avenue
Park Ridge, Illinois 60068
Silver accessories

Metal City Findings Corp.
450 W. 31st Street
New York, New York 10001

The Miniature Mart & Peddlers
Shop
883 39th Avenue
San Francisco, California 94121
Silver

J. J. Morris Co.
394 Elm Street
Southbridge, Massachusetts 01550
Tiny brass screws

Bill Muller Wooden Toys
Rockhill Industrial Park
87 Commerce Drive
Telford, Pennsylvania 18969
Pewter items

Something Different Miniatures
PO Box 1628 FDR Station
New York, New York 10022
Country tin

Taylor House
Bench & Perry Streets
Galena, Illinois 61036
Filigree metal items

Taylor Made Tines
5030 Raton Circle
Long Beach, California 90807
Pewter pieces

The Village Smithy
73 Kensington Road
Bronxville, New York 10708
Lanterns, fencing and gates,
kitchen utensils, hinges, hooks,
balconies, benches, accessories

William J. Weder Enterprises
Upper Black Eddy RD #1
Pennsylvania 18972
Hand-forged lanterns
Candlestands
Hinges
Wall hangers

MILLWORK

The Workshop
424 No. Broadview
Wichita, Kansas 67208
Millwork and cabinetry

MINIATURE BOOKS AND BOOKBINDING

Mr. Bela Blau
A-1 Bookbinding
110 West Pico Boulevard
Los Angeles, California 90015
Bookbinding of miniature books

Dawson's Book Shop
535 North Larchmont Blvd.
Los Angeles, California 90004
Rare books, old and new

The Miniature Book Studio
Box 2603
Lakewood, Ohio 44107

Minutiques
82b Trafalgar Street
Brighton BN 1
4 EB Sussex, England

MISCELLANEOUS

Hermania Anslinger
320 South Ralph Street
Spokane, Washington 99202
Carvings
Animals
Figures

Arlene's Memories in Miniature
5521 East Morris
Wichita, Kansas 67218
Doll bonnets

Artfoam
100 East Montauk Highway
Lindenhurst, New York 11757
Artfoam, a carvable, rigid,
polyurethane foam

Beehive Studio
826 Deerfield Road
Deerfield, Illinois 60015
Miniature labels

James Bliss & Company
Dedham, Massachusetts 02026
Linen rigging thread for
rushing

Connoisseur Studio, Inc.
Box 7187
Louisville, Kentucky 40207
Acrylic paints
Decoupage materials
Varnishes

D & E Miniatures
PO Box 2117
Culver City, California 90230
Straw items
Teddy bears
German import wood miniatures

A. and S. Grainger
613 Oxford House Emanuel
Ann Arbor, Michigan 48104
   Billiard table
   Marionette theatre

J. Hermes
Box 23
El Monte, California 91734
   Cigar box house kits

J H B Imports, Inc.
2131 South Jasmine Street
Denver, Colorado 80222
   Clock faces

Nancy Lee's Miniatures
379 103rd Avenue
Plainwell, Michigan 49080
   Food items

Jane E. McCandless
Dog River Road
RD #2
Montpelier, Vermont 05602
   Watercolor paintings
   Oil paintings
   Hand-painted trays

Microbius
534 Red Haw Road
Dayton, Ohio 45405
   Food items
   Teddy bears

The Mouse Hole
111 Eagle Rock Avenue
Roseland, New Jersey 07068
   Baker foods

Bill Muller Wooden Toys
Rockhill Industrial Park
87 Commerce Drive
Telford, Pennsylvania 18969
   Oil paintings

New York Bronze Powder Company
515 Dowd Avenue
Elizabeth, New Jersey 07201
   No-Vue window frosting

Pickwick Miniatures
PO Box 297
Glenview, Illinois 60025
   Fireplaces
   Linens

B. Shackman & Co.
85 Fifth Avenue
New York, New York 10003
   Red square patio bricks
   Magazines
   Telephones

Pamela White Miniatures
12 Rutland Square
Boston, Massachusetts 02118
   Hand-painted murals
   Pictures
   Shadow boxes

MOLD MATERIALS

Dow Corning Corp.
Midland, Michigan 48640
   RTV silicone "Silastic" mold
      materials
   "Silastic" 740 adhesives

General Electric Co.
1 River Road
Schenectady, New York 12306
   RTV silicone mold materials
   Mastic adhesives

Transene Co., Inc.
Route 1
Rowley, Massachusetts 01969
   Silicast ®, silicone elastomer
      systems: Silicast 10-for epoxy;
      Silicast 20 for polyester; Silicast
      30 for polyurethane

NEEDLEWORK

Boutique Margot
26 West 54th Street
New York, New York 10019
   Silk gauze for petit point size 38

June E. Doll
PO Box 147
Rockville, Connecticut 06066
   Cross-stitch kits
   Samplers

Rene and Judy Gaillardetz
PO Box 575
Marlboro, Massachusetts 01732
   Miniature needlework
   Fine crochet
   Tapestries
   Petit point rugs

Jean Jessop
64 Blackburn Road
Summit, New Jersey 07901
   Tapestries for collectors

Jane E. McCandless
Dog River Road RD #2
Montpelier, Vermont 05602

Old Curiosity Shop
Mobery Lake
British Columbia, Canada
   Quilts
   Afghans

The Warner House
Box 895
Portsmouth, New Hampshire 03801
   Mini samplers

PACKAGED POLYESTER CASTING RESINS

California Titan Products
2501 Birch Street
Santa Ana, California 92707
   *Polyester resin and contingent
      supplies sold in small
      quantities*

Deep Flex Plastic Molds, Inc.
2740 Lipscomb Street
Fort Worth, Texas 76110

Industrial Plastic Supply Co.
324 Canal Street
New York, New York 10013
   *Wide range of plastic materials,
      including resins, fillers,
      reinforcements, etc., all
      quantities available*

Taylor and Art Plastics
1710 East 12th Street
Oakland, California 94606

Valspar Corp.
200 Sayre Street
Rockford, Illinois 61101

PATTERNS

Elspeth Originals
7404 Helmsdale Road
Bethesda, Maryland 20034
   Patterns for dollhouse rooms

Green Door Studio
Dept. NN
517 E. Annapolis Street
St. Paul, Minnesota 55118
   *Patterns for country store and
      dollhouse furniture*

PLASTER

Pure Pac Corp.
200 Elmora Avenue
Elizabeth, New Jersey 07202
   May be purchased at local store

PLASTIC MATERIALS AND TILES (FUSIBLE)

Poly-Dec Company, Inc.
PO Box 541
Bayonne, New Jersey 07002
   *Poly-Mosaic ® tiles, versatile
      heat-fusible, gluable, 3/4"
      square tiles, transparent in
      stained glass colors*
   *Dec-Ets—fusible plastic pellets in
      9 colors*

PLASTIC POLISHES AND COMPOUNDS

Hyprex Diamond Compounds
Engis Corporation
8035 N. Austin Avenue
Morton Grove, Illinois 60053
   *Full range of diamond-based
      polishing compounds and
      polishing cloths*

Matchless Metal Polish Co.
Glen Ridge, New Jersey 07028
   *Domet flannel buffs with one row
      of sewing. Coarse, fast-cutting
      compound: Matchless #327 and
      #962. Medium cutting,
      medium finish: Tripoli #114,
      Triple XXX Diamond*

3M Company
St. Paul, Minnesota 55101
   *Three-M-ite ® resin-bond cloth
      belts, aluminum oxide sanding
      belts, grit sixes 80 and 100 for
      dry sanding only*
   Wet-or-dry Tri-M-ite paper

PLASTIC PUTTIES

Atlas Minerals and Chemicals
  Division
ESB, Inc.
Mertztown, Pennsylvania 19539
  *Two-part claylike epoxy putty
    adhesive in various colors*

Devcon Corp.
Danvers, Massachusetts 01923
  Plastic steel and epoxy bond

Polyform Products, Inc.
9420 Byron Street
Schiller Park, Illinois 60176
  *A modeling plastic that stays soft
    until heated to 275° F. for 15–30
    minutes
  Polyform*

Sculpmetal Co.
701 Investment Building
Pittsburgh, Pennsylvania 15222
  Plastic steel and epoxy bond

Woodhill Chemical Co.
18731 Cranwood Parkway
Cleveland, Ohio 44128
  *Duro-plastic, Aluminum, Liquid
    Steel, Gook ®, Celastic ®*

POLYESTERS

American Cyanamid Co.
Plastics and Resins Division
Wallingford, Connecticut 06492
  Laminac®

Diamond Shamrock Chemical Co.
300 Union Commerce Building
Cleveland, Ohio 44115
  *Excellent water-clear all-purpose
    casting resin—Dion 6914*

PPG Industries, Inc.
Coatings and Resins Division
One Gateway Center
Pittsburgh, Pennsylvania 15222
  Selectron®

Reichhold Chemicals, Inc.
RCI Building
White Plains, New York 10602
  Polylite ® 32-032, etc.

Alec Tiranti, Ltd.
70 High Street
Theale, Berkshire
England

RESINS AND SHEETING–ACRYLIC

Ain Plastics
65 Fourth Avenue
New York, New York 10003
  *A wide range of sheets, resins,
    and plastic findings*

Cadillac Plastic
148 Parkway
Kalamazoo, Michigan 49006
  Outlets throughout the country

Imperial Chemicals Industries, Ltd.
Plastics Division
Welwyn Garden City
Herts, England

Industrial Plastics
324 Canal Street
New York, New York 10013
  *Jobber of a large assortment of
    resins, sheetings, fillers,
    findings, etc.*

Rohm and Haas Company
6th and Market Streets
Philadelphia, Pennsylvania 19106
  *Plexiglas, MMMA monomer,
    Rhoplex, AC-33 Acrysol GS,
    Tamol 731, Acryloid B7,B72*

Alec Tiranti, Ltd.
70 High Street
Theale, Berkshire, England

Vistron Corp.
12335 S. Van Ness Avenue
Hawthorne, California 90250
  *Silmar S40, S41, water-clear
    polyester resins*

RESINS AND SHEETING–EPOXY

Atlas Minerals and Chemicals
Mertztown, Pennsylvania 19539
  *Moldable two-part epoxy putty
  Epoxy bond*

Dow Chemical Co.
Midland, Michigan 48640
DER 332 and DOW

John W. McNabb Laboratories
313–317 E. Fulton Street
Lancaster, Pennsylvania 17604
*Soft epoxy dough in two parts:
cures at room temperature to
be buttered on a form or used
as an adhesive: called McNabb*

Marblette Corp.
37-31 30th Street
Long Island City, New York 11101
Marblette ®

Ren Plastics
5656 S. Cedar Street
Lansing, Michigan 48909
*Epoxy two-part clear system
RP-106/H-953*

Shell Chemical Co.
Industrial Chemicals Division
110 W. 51st Street
New York, New York 10020
Epon ®

Tra-Con, Inc.
55 North Street
Medford, Massachusetts 02155
*Clear casting epoxy system
Tra-Cast* ® *3012*

ROOMS–SHADOW BOXES

Bassett Antiques
7102 Stanton Avenue
Buena Park, California 90620
Rooms

The Beehive Studio
826 Deerfield Road
Deerfield, Illinois 60015
Rooms

Carlson's Custom Crafts
671 Bender Lane
West Chicago, Illinois 60185
*Wholesale manufacturer of
furniture and room boxes*

The Doll House Factory
Box 456, 157 Main Street
Lebanon, New Jersey 08833
Shadow boxes

Dolphin Originals
Robert Bernhard
7302 Hasbrook Avenue
Philadelphia, Pennsylvania 19111
Rooms to order

John Flint
600 Davis Street
Evanston, Illinois 60201
Rooms

The Lilliput Shop
5955 S W 179th Avenue
Beaverton, Oregon 97005
Shadow box rooms

Mark Mallus
702 S. Division Street
Ann Arbor, Michigan 48104
Shadow boxes

Nor-Med Miniatures
8248 N. Kenton Avenue
Skokie, Illinois 60076
*Miniature rooms
Vignettes*

Braxton Payne
60 Fifth Street, NE
Atlanta, Georgia 30308
Lighted display rooms

Rena Potect
PO Box 92
Steeleville, Illinois 62288

Pamela White Miniatures
12 Rutland Square
Boston, Massachusetts 02118
Shadow boxes

Winbon Creations
3900 Paradise Drive
Tiburon, California 94920
*Custom rooms
Shadow boxes*

Woody Creek Workshop
38 W. 487 Burr Road Lane
St. Charles, Illinois 60174
*Custom-made miniature rooms
Vignettes*

Yesterday's Rooms
111 Groveland Street
Haverhill, Massachusetts 01830
Period settings in miniatures

A. & J. Zasadil, Arkwrights
50 Cedar Lane
Lincolnshire, Illinois 60015
Custom rooms on special order

RUGS AND
RUG PATTERNS

D. Bosse
2040 Greenwood Drive
San Carlos, California 94070
Rug patterns

Chestnut Hill Studio
Box 38
Churchville, New York 14428
Rugs

Rene and Judy Gaillardetz
PO Box 575
Marlboro, Massachusetts 01732
Petit point rugs

A. and S. Grainger
613 Oxford House Emanuel
Ann Arbor, Michigan 48104
Braided rugs

Jean Jessop
64 Blackburn Road
Summit, New Jersey 07901
Petit point rugs

Jane E. McCandless
Dog River Road, RD #2
Montpelier, Vermont 05602
Hooked rugs

Kate P. Marks
11 West Street
Albany, New York 12206
Petit point rugs

The Miniature Mart & Peddlers
  Shop
Dept. NN
883 39th Avenue
San Francisco, California 94121

Bill Muller Wooden Toys
Rockhill Industrial Park
87 Commerce Drive
Telford, Pennsylvania 18969
Oriental rugs

Old Curiosity Shop
Mobery Lake
British Columbia, Canada
Braided rugs

Something Different Miniatures
PO Box 1628 FDR Station
New York, New York 10022
Victorian rugs

Pamela White Miniatures
12 Rutland Square
Boston, Massachusetts 02118
Oriental rugs

SOLVENTS

Shell Chemical Co.
110 W. 51st Street
New York, New York 10020
  Acetone

Union Carbide Co.
Chemicals and Plastics Division
270 Park Avenue
New York, New York 10017

TOOLS—SEE "MACHINES
AND TOOLS"

WALLPAPER

Joe Hermes
10113 Whitmore Street
El Monte, California 91733

Nancy Lee's Miniatures
379 103rd Avenue
Plainwell, Michigan 49080

The Miniature Mart & Peddlers
  Shop
Dept. NN
883 39th Avenue
San Francisco, California 94121

The Mouse Hole
111 Eagle Rock Avenue
Roseland, New Jersey 07068

Bill Muller Wooden Toys
Rockhill Industrial Park
87 Commerce Drive
Telford, Pennsylvania 18969

Pamela White Miniatures
12 Rutland Square
Boston, Massachusetts 02118

Willoughby's Eighteenth Century
PO Box 918
Los Altos, California 94022

WELDING

A. Atkins
73 Kensington Road
Bronxville, New York 10708
  Blacksmith

Weder Enterprises
Box 176 Route 1
Upper Black Eddy, Pennsylvania
18972
Welding

WOOD

Albert Constantine & Sons, Inc.
2050 Eastchester Road
Bronx, New York 10461
Wood and wood inlays

Craftsman Wood Service Co.
2272 South Mary Street
Chicago, Illinois 60608

Elliott Bay Lumber Co.
16 So. Spokane Street
Seattle, Washington 96134
Thermo wood tape

The Lilliput Shop
5955 SW 179th Avenue
Beaverton, Oregon 97005
Cabinet woods

The Miniature Mart &
   Peddlers Shop
Dept. NN
883 39th Avenue
San Francisco, California 94121
Doors
Moldings

Northeastern Scale Molds Inc.
P.O. Box 425
Methuen, Massachusetts 01844

Pamela White Miniatures
12 Rutland Square
Boston, Massachusetts 02118
Parquet floors

Willoughby's Eighteenth Century
PO Box 918
Los Altos, California 94022
Paneling

Index

(*Italic* figures refer to illustrations.)